It's a set time of favor
... beauty for ashes ....
blessing instead of mourning.
You are called by the
Lord to be a mighty oak
tree who can, through
Him, rebuild, restore
& renew every place
on your path..
Isaiah 61: 1-4

Yvonne Denise

Yvonne has lovingly chronicled her journey as a prophetic intercessor. If you've *ever* desired the seer anointing, this will whet your appetite and draw you to the table!

Carolyn Parr
Founder, Sing Your Song Ministries
Former missionary to Turkey

An Oak of Righteousness: Grafting the Seeds of Destiny into the Root of Covenant is a *must-read* for anyone who has the privilege of working with marginalized communities. As one who works with people who are homeless or in extreme poverty scenarios, I am daily faced with the messiness and harsh realities of life that people are confronted with. Neglect, sexual abuse, mental health illnesses, drug abuse, job loss, depression, death, hopelessness. Real people with very real issues. Yvonne's writings inspire and even challenge me to view people and their current state in life from an Isaiah 61 lens. Through all of the dirt and all of our imperfections and failures, He's safely hidden our destinies. He makes an exchange that transforms us into something beautiful and then firmly establishes us as strong and magnificent oak trees where we were previously unstable in every way! It was a part of His plan from the very beginning!

So if you feel like your life is a mess or you're daily dealing with people who seem to be beyond repair, remember God is all for fixer uppers! There is HOPE! As Yvonne shares her life journey of being grafted into covenant, you will be inspired to see yourself and others through the scope of God's original intent… that we would all be oaks of righteousness, the Lord's planting for the purpose of rebuilding, restoring and renewing families, communities and nations. My prayer is that these Spirit-breathed writings would come alive in your heart as you read in a way that brings breakthrough in your perspective.

Adrienne C. Threatt
Co-Founder & Executive Director, Hope Vibes Inc.
Co-Founder, GiveHopeDaily & Hope Unleashed

Imagine being on a road called Purpose that takes you through peaks, valleys, and mountainous terrains, only to arrive at this beautiful, quaint little town called Destiny. Well, *An Oak of Righteousness: Grafting the Seeds of Destiny into the Root of Covenant* walks you through Yvonne's adventurous journey with God. It's an example of how well God plans our lives for His kingdom purposes. *An Oak of Righteousness* is your GET IT GOING apostolic trumpet sound for what God has empowered and equipped you to do. This book is a MUST have in your spiritual arsenal.

Susan C. Napier
Author of *The Pre-Birth Briefing*
Pastor, First Love Ministries
Founder, Mommas Inc.

Adorned with thankfulness to God and His Son Jesus Christ, Yvonne Denise looks fearlessly at her own history and at our shared history as the redeemed of the Lord. With eyes wide open to heavenly guidance and help, she writes *An Oak of Righteousness: Grafting the Seeds of Destiny into the Root of Covenant* encouraging and outlining a way forward to joyously and effectively minister the gospel in our communities. Read it and dance!

Karen Zika
Board of Directors, Statesville Upper Room Ministry

As believers, we know how essential it is to live a life that is led by Holy Spirit. As educators, we know the importance and power of history. *An Oak of Righteousness: Grafting the Seeds of Destiny into the Root of Covenant* is a convergence of both as Yvonne Denise takes you on a journey through the Word of God, human history and her personal conversations with Holy Spirit. As you read the testimonies of how the Lord answers the prayer of the hungry heart, you will also sense how your life is an important part of what the Lord wants to do in the earth today. Dive into this book and hear the voice of Holy Spirit. Your heart will be stirred and challenged.

Kevin and Rosemerry Blash
Daystar Arising Academy

An Oak of RIGHTEOUSNESS

Grafting the Seeds of Destiny into the Root of Covenant

YVONNE DENISE

Foreword by Linda Heidler

ISBN: 978-1-54397-052-4 (print)

ISBN: 978-1-54397-053-1 (ebook)

Dedication

I dedicate this book to My Reality—Father, Jesus (Son) and Holy Spirit; My spiritual father—Chuck Pierce, Glory of Zion International and Global Spheres, Inc.; My Releasing Heaven Ministries Family; the Lord's Triumphant Reserve, the Prodigals, and other 11th Hour saints hidden everywhere!

Special Thanks and Acknowledgments

Special thanks to Susan Napier, Adrienne Threatt, Jayne Hood, My Street Team, and Linda Heidler for their prayers and encouragement.

Special Acknowledgements: Editors Karen Zika and Lynda P. Myers, Artist Eva Crawford, Embassy of Zion, the Coastline Prayer Team, Hearts on Fire Fellowship, as always, my sister Chellie, and my spiritual mom Ann Strickland.

CONTENTS

FOREWORD

Most people grow up asking, "Who am I? Why am I here? Where am I going?" Unfortunately, many are still asking those questions well into adulthood. In her book, *An Oak of Righteousness: Grafting the Seeds of Destiny into the Root of Covenant*, Yvonne Denise reveals a path to answer those questions.

The key to unlocking the answers is in covenant. Yvonne lays a solid foundation of Biblical revelation concerning covenant. Beginning in Genesis with God's covenant with Abraham, Yvonne traces the extension of covenant to a family, a tribe, a nation and ultimately to the world, culminating with the Gentiles from all nations being grafted into the very covenant God made with one man, Abraham.

She brings out, from the example of Israel's covenant relationship with God, many of the basic principles of covenant. Our failures do not negate God's faithfulness. Covenant is a very secure relationship. Time does not expire on God's covenant promises. He is faithful forever, as evidenced by the existence of the nation of Israel today.

As He called Abraham into a covenant relationship with Him and gave him a new identity and destiny, He does the same for each of us. Within this covenant relationship with God, identity and destiny can be discovered.

Through telling her personal life story, Yvonne brings to reality the process of discovering your own identity and living out your own destiny. Beginning with her childhood, she relates how God was working in her and through others to bring her into an understanding of covenant and the unfolding of her life's purpose.

The telling of her story is very real and relatable. You will find yourself identifying with her struggles and confusion. You will understand how she feels when things do not turn out the way she expected, when she takes a wrong turn and has to get back on track and when she feels that her desires will never be fulfilled. You will also marvel with her at the intricate ways in which God weaves His Biblical promises with our personal promises to bring fulfilment to all His promises.

She has a testimony of overcoming, of maturing faith, of living in the identity God gave her and of fulfilling the destiny He created for her. Her story will encourage you to keep believing all that God has said to you and to keep moving through the next door that He opens.

My prayer for you as you read this book is that you will receive life changing revelation about covenant, that you will enter into a personal covenant relationship with God, and that through that relationship you will find the answers to who you are, why you are here and where you are going. May you become an Oak of Righteousness whose seeds of destiny are grafted into the root of covenant.

Linda Heidler

THEME SCRIPTURE IN ISAIAH

Isaiah 61:1-4 (NIV): The Spirit of the Sovereign LORD is on me, because the LORD has anointed me to proclaim good news to the poor. He has sent me to bind up the brokenhearted, to proclaim freedom for the captives and release from darkness for the prisoners, to proclaim the year of the LORD's favor and the day of vengeance of our God, to comfort all who mourn, and provide for those who grieve in Zion—to bestow on them a crown of beauty instead of ashes, the oil of joy instead of mourning, and a garment of praise instead of a spirit of despair. **They will be called oaks**

of righteousness, a planting of the LORD for the display of his splendor. They will rebuild the ancient ruins and restore the places long devastated; they will renew the ruined cities that have been devastated for generations.

An Oak Tree

An oak tree is a thing of great beauty, great strength and longevity. Its roots are the first part of the tree that grow. Its trunk is tough and can store water so it can survive drought, storms, and even fires. If an oak tree is cut down, its roots can sprout again. Its crown of branches, leaves, and acorns provide shelter and food for many different species of animals including insects. It also provides for other plant life. The wind that blows through its leaves helps it to pollinate and produce fruit. It is a tree of the generations as some types can live from 200 to 1000 years.

PART ONE:

Introduction—A Call to Renew Ruined Cities

CHAPTER 1

Walking Through the Devastation of a Generation

WHEN I BEGAN MY JOURNEY WITH THE LORD, I FELT that I was the least likely to be used by Him in any significant way, much like Gideon in Judges 6. When I was born, my family lived in a small apartment above a doctor's office in West Philadelphia. Segregation was still in full effect: although there were businesses owned by different races just a half-block away, all of my neighbors were black. From my young perspective, that fact did not make us less in any way. Folks in the neighborhood were in various professions, many lived in houses, and several had cars. Our family doctor was around the corner. We could easily walk to the essentials for any child: my paternal grandmother's house, the grocery store, my school, the library, the candy store, and the park.

My family fell into the blue-collar working class. I did not really focus much on possessions until I began to notice differences at school. I found that our economic status made a difference in what I could or could not do. We did not have the extra money for dance or music lessons or for some of the class trips. Racially speaking, I found out that there were certain places either that we could not go to, such as the privately-held amusement parks, or that we were not really welcome at. However, I considered our trips to my mother's hometown of Baltimore to be its own adventure. Most times we rode the train— which had to be just like riding one of those roller coasters. Then when we eventually owned a car, we had a whole state to visit called "Mary-Land" with its own big house right off the highway.

Although both of my grandmothers were saved and faithfully serving the Lord, my parents were not. Of note, neither of my parents' fathers had played an active role in their lives. We did not attend church together as a family; to the contrary, there was actually trouble at home. About a year ago, I finally watched the movie Concussion and quickly texted my sister that I thought that was what was wrong with our dad. She agreed; our dad had played semi-pro football in the 50s with very little safety padding. He then contracted spinal meningitis working for the Water Department when I was two. He had quite a number of violent outbursts throughout the rest of his life. I just learned to live on high alert with *one eye open* throughout most nights.

Thankfully, there was a neighbor's daughter who took us to Sunday School at the church on the corner. I remember having the biggest bible ever on the coffee table, and I remember loving going to church. I loved hearing about Jesus who loved all the little children regardless of the color of their skin. I remember always going to that big book and being so delighted to find the same Scripture text there that been taught or preached. Even what Jesus said was clearly written there in red ink. Those were the days of the Civil Rights Movement and Rev. Dr. Martin Luther King, Jr. **I longed to one day preach the gospel as Dr. King did so I could bring about change too.** I loved Dr. King's dream of living in a world free of the negative external distinctions. I believe it was a dream, a vision given to him by God and one rooted deeply in that big book, the written Scriptures.

However, by age 15, I found myself willfully turning from the Lord. I no longer saw the church actively engaged in the community, and I did not see the behavior of "church folk" differing radically from the behavior of most other neighbors. Growing up during the Civil Rights Movement set the bar of expectation pretty high for me. During my younger years, the church was involved in the marches and they anchored the activity around helping people in very tangible ways. Unfortunately, that activity often ended in violence. In addition to the violence in response to the Movement, tragically there were assassinations: first President Kennedy, then Dr. King, and then Senator Kennedy. Interspersed in those tragedies were a missile crisis, the Cold War, and then the Vietnam War. I remember the air raid drills at school, the news reports, and the riots. It is quite something to live in that level of trauma. No one felt safe even walking to the corner store. Stores and buildings were burned out and random acts of violence sprang up everywhere. One Pennsylvania newspaper reported that between June 1963 and May 1968, our cities witnessed 239 riots involving over 200,000 participants. Eight thousand people were injured and 190 lost their lives.

I remember driving through Memphis in 1995 and being determined not to stop there. And I could still feel the trauma at the grassy knoll in Dallas when my brother drove me by there in 2012. "Darkness cannot drive out darkness; only light can do that. Hate cannot drive out hate, only love can do that." Dr. King, 1957.

When I was nine, as my father feared what the riots would mean for our attending school that fall, my family suddenly moved from West Philadelphia to Southwest Philadelphia. To our despair, he was not very communicative about his plans; so, after my sister and I visited my maternal grandmother in Baltimore for two weeks in the summer of 1968, we unexpectedly came back home to an entirely different neighborhood. We never even had the opportunity to say goodbye to our friends. Years later, my sister ran into one of those friends, and she was so glad to reconnect, because it had seemed to her that we had vanished. During that time, I also started a new school. It was what would be called a magnet school today. I had to travel there by public transportation, three hours daily. My mother took me for a few weeks before she had to go to work and then I was on my own. After school, I had to meet her at her job in Center City Philadelphia so we could travel home together. During the next eight years, I simply fell in love with our city as I ended up walking quite a bit. I passed government buildings, the newspaper building, a major hospital, churches, historic sites, businesses, department stores, and even City Hall where the statue of William Penn sat. By the time I was 12, my mother had changed jobs and I was completely on my own. I then was able to travel a different route past the Parkway where the various museums were, and the city's Main Library became my library. My dad instilled within me a love for history and would often say, "If you know your history, the sense of who you really are can never be taken away from you." The city itself became my living classroom. In addition, I was able to meet students of many different nationalities and backgrounds, even the children of some dignitaries. Many of these later became very successful in their chosen careers.

Moreover, in the midst of all of that, there was the hippie movement, which brought its own layer of chaos. There was also the typical awkwardness of my teenage years. And there were assaults that I faced alone for many years. When there is trouble at home, children are vulnerable to predators. I was withdrawn and did not seem to fit in anywhere – with family or at school, or at church. I survived by reading and diving into my schoolwork, but my internal pain grew. Starting at age 12, I began to feel that the Bible as written had lost its power and its relevance, both for our community and for me personally. It just seemed logical that God simply needed to change to keep up with the times. (I know there are those same sentiments stirring today, but I have found that the Lord already has set in motion the answers needed.)

So, when I graduated from high school at age 17 and started college, I completely stepped out of the boat of a church-centered life. I determined that I would simply worship the Lord in my own way. Needless to say, by the time I responded to His wooing me back, I was VERY broken. After just a few months of being out of the boat, even at an Ivy League school, like a frog placed in slowly boiling water, I increasingly became immersed in a world of partying—drinking, drugs, and full-out sexual sin. At the start of my sophomore year, I began to have panic attacks as even more social disconnects happened. I barely managed to keep going due to some very serious missteps. Before I turned 19, I had Student Health give me an EKG because my heart felt like it was just racing all of the time. Their recommendation was to leave school; however, that simply was not an option. A good education was my family's dream—it was seemingly all I had been groomed to do. In our Western culture, without specific talent to act, sing, dance, or play sports, college was believed to be the only absolute ticket to a better life. Consequently, I pressed on with more drugs, more drinking; and I quietly hoped for an answer. I even joined the University Gospel Choir while I limped to class and through my extracurricular activities. Amazingly, I kept a decent GPA and was even selected to be a part of the Onyx Senior Honor Society, but I was numb on the inside until. . .

CHAPTER 2

No Respecter of Persons— Receiving a Crown of Beauty

ALTHOUGH I FELL IN LOVE WITH JESUS AT A YOUNG age, I didn't come to a saving knowledge of Him, as in a verbal confession acknowledging that I needed to be saved and the actual acceptance of the great exchange of His glory for my sin and shame, until I was almost 22. I cannot recall ever hearing about those simple steps before then.

It is a wonder how sometimes we feel powerless when that is not so with the God of All Creation. What we believe and what we say matters to Him. Our own voice can change the course of our eternal future. If we believe who Jesus is according to Scripture and we say that we want to follow Him, that is all that is needed. Wow!

I was at a very broken place when at a Friday night prayer meeting, I heard this young mother talk about Jesus with the same love I remembered as a little girl. She had such joy and such peace. I determined that whatever it took, I wanted what she had. So, I said a quiet prayer in my heart. I knew this young mother only because I ended up at her house several times for Sunday lunch after church service. Towards the end of my senior year of college, I had seemingly stumbled upon this community choir that was based out of her church. I had organized a Gospelrama for one of the college groups that I was a part of. Someone told me about this choir and I invited them to participate. When they sang, they dramatized their songs with motion and it completely drew me in. I remember growing up having great fun pretending to be the Supremes, the Temptations, the Monkees, and the Jackson 5. And, here was a group using dance and drama to actually worship the Lord.

I somehow was emboldened to pursue joining this choir. I reached out to them with my desire, letting them know that, although I was not a great singer, I knew I could hold my part, and I promised to faithfully practice. The choir's founding director graciously agreed. There were a couple of others from my college who also joined. We started making the trek together to attend choir practice. There was no direct public transportation so it meant a serious walk off-campus through an unknown neighborhood. I soon found myself attending some Sunday services with the choir director, and then the Friday night prayer meetings as well. I immediately noted how the pews were full on Sundays with well over 300 people, but this Friday night prayer meeting only had about 25 in attendance. But, none of that mattered, as I was now at a place of hope.

I "went forward" at the altar call for prayer that very Sunday after being touched by the young mother's testimony that Friday evening. When I said I was there for salvation, the elders met with me privately to explain what I was committing to and to make sure I knew what I was asking for. They told me the simple steps to salvation and I prayed that prayer. They directed me that I needed to be water baptized, which I promptly did, and my journey of the Lord's putting my fractured pieces back together began. Just thinking about how broken I was back then still brings tears to my eyes. His saving grace was truly through and through—past, present, and future.

Shortly after this, I was introduced to being "baptized by fire." Our choir's drama director invited me to dinner at her house and talked to me about the strength that the separate baptism of Holy Spirit brought. She then handed me a little book and a bible and left me alone in a quiet room. Before closing the door, she said if I wanted this baptism, she would pray with me. I found all the Scriptures contained in the little book were in the bible, and I told her that I absolutely wanted that, as I needed all the help I could get. So we prayed together, I asked Jesus to baptize me with Holy Spirit, and He did! A River of Life began to flow through me as I released unknown tongues!

I was in graduate school at this time, and I quickly discovered that an academic social work program was not the Lord's training plan for me. Consequently, I was not able to stay much longer at the church or with the choir as traveling distance and circumstances shifted. It took me several years to find a church that fully believed what the Scriptures said. After moving back home, I started attending the new church that came to our family's neighborhood, but I found out after a year that the pastor believed that the Virgin birth that brought Jesus was mystical and not a real event. I did not quite know how to handle that, so I stopped going. I then bought a house just outside of Philadelphia and started attending the church of some folks who had come knocking on my door. After six months there, they told me that Holy Spirit, whom I personally communicated with daily, no longer functioned and that healing was not for today. Again, I did not know how to handle that, so I went to the Lord in prayer and told Him I would go only where He sent me. It would take another three and a half years to find a believing church. I spent that time reading the Word and watching some very good Christian programming. I was temporarily fed by Marilyn Hickey, Joyce Meyer and others, plus I read books by ministers such as Andrew Murray, Kenneth Hagin, and Derek Prince. I also read books about great intercessors, such as Rees Howell, and about past Revivals.

Throughout the entire time since my baptism in Holy Spirit, I discovered that through Holy Spirit, I could ask questions and receive answers. Jesus said that Holy Spirit would teach us and He does. Sometimes the answers would come in the words of Scripture that would suddenly jump out at me; sometimes I would have a dream; sometimes I would have a knowing; sometimes there would be a still small internal voice; sometimes I would get a word from someone else either directly or through a teaching or through what I came to know as a prophetic demonstration or through a seemingly random conversation; and just a few times, I heard an audible voice. I also learned first-hand that there were both angels and demons as I spent a good bit of time getting delivered from my prodigal past. Moreover, I had dreams of people groups. In my dreams, I would see the first peoples of what looked like the Pacific Isles. I would find myself in what looked like a rice patty in Vietnam. Then there were people I could not quite place, whom I later came to meet in 2015.

Before long, a family member came to announce that he had found THE church. I was skeptical, so I went to his birthday celebration and met the pastors there. I casually grilled them with my list of questions concerning what they believed. Once I satisfactorily received all the answers I needed, I promised to be at their church the next day.

I then spent the next four years at this amazing little storefront church that was nestled in a neighborhood inundated with gangs, drugs, and a poverty mentality. All of the billboards were alcohol-related, and across the street was a crack house. We were only 50-60 people strong on any given Sunday, but our pastor was a passionate, spirit-filled believer. And we were indeed a house of prayer. We prayer-walked the community, knocked on doors to pray with our neighbors and had early Wednesday morning prayer as well as Friday night prayer. We even voluntarily added a Morning Prayer call chain. A long-time family friend became my spiritual mom in the process, and we spent many Sunday afternoons and evenings in worship and prayer at her house. I had a standing invitation to spend the night, as sometimes it was just too good to leave. Also, anytime we heard about prayer shut-ins at other churches, we were all in. Those were also the days of house revival meetings and you would often find well-known spiritual leaders in the living rooms of the saints. Those meetings were typically packed with folks wall-to-wall. We felt blessed if we could even stand the entire time on the basement steps just to receive a drop of their anointing.

It was in that season and through 2010 that I heard from the Lord about my call into five-fold ministry. He confirmed that call in numerous ways, including confirming prophecies from other active ministers. I sensed a call to intercession, and I heard at various times, "I call you to preach!", "I call you as a prophet," "You are a prophet with an apostolic anointing," and in a corrective tone, "I called you as a watchman." All of these calls are tied together. In the Hebrew, there are several words that reflect the call of the prophet. Roeh means Seer, describing one who sees things supernaturally. Chozeh means a vision that speaks. Nataph means an anointing of decrees that open the heavens. Then Shamar is the watchman prophet who is linked to harvest. Shamar is the word that the Lord used with Adam when He directed him to watch over the garden. I was so honored to have the Lord speak to me and to call me into His service.

We are actually all called to minister. There is the Scripture in Jeremiah that says that the Lord has a plan and purpose for us even before He put us in our mother's womb. And, He is no respecter of persons. The Scriptures say that there is neither Jew nor Gentile, neither slave nor free, nor is there male and female, for you are all one in Christ Jesus. If you belong to Christ, then you are Abraham's seed and heirs according to the promise. (Galatians 3:28-29, NIV) These words are sure and true. Walking that out amongst other believers, however, can be a challenge. I came up in the Lord at a time when there was not much support for women ministers, especially those who were single, Spirit-filled, unrelated to a lineage of ministers, and who did not attend a bible school or seminary. Moreover, if your call was not that of a pastor, your position was considered less than. However, the Lord has strongly encouraged me by His Spirit. I have had profound encounters with the Scriptures in Jeremiah and in Ezekiel in terms of the watchman calling. Especially firm was the call to uproot and to tear down, to build and to plant, the accountability to expediently issue the warnings received, and for calling forth the Wind of the Spirit to raise up the dry bones in His body to become an army fit for His use. (Please note that I do not espouse replacement theology in any form. As you will see in the chapters that follow, I stand on the Scriptures that declare that we have instead been grafted into God's covenant with His first nation. The Lord has used Israel as a powerful signpost of His faithfulness to "watch over His Word to perform it" (Jeremiah 1:12, paraphrased), to establish His kingdom, and, as a root of covenant, to bless other nations. Jesus came to fulfill that covenant and extend it to completely wipe away our sin by the power of His blood.)

One of the ultimate honors from the Lord for me occurred during one of our Ephesians 4 Movement (E4M) Equipping Services in 2016. That was the year I began to see knighted angels. I and several from our team had been meditating about our new angelic company and what their presence meant. I even found confirmation about these angels from Chuck Pierce's book, <u>A Time to Triumph</u>. Then, during the E4M service, I saw the Lord enter with some of those angels and place a crown of garland on my head. I struggled with receiving that at first as I consider my life laid down before the Lord as a bond-servant. I later repented as I realized the Lord was indicating that there was a shift in season. One of the things that was about to be fulfilled was a trip to Northern Iraq (modern day Assyria) to visit the previously unidentified people in my dreams.

In the last couple of months since the Lord has released me to write this book, the Scripture in Isaiah 61:3 (NIV) is at the forefront of my thoughts: "to bestow on them **a crown of beauty** (garland in some translations) **instead of ashes**, the oil of joy instead of mourning, and a garment of praise instead of a spirit of despair. **They will be called oaks of righteousness, a planting of the Lord for the display of his splendor."** That is the Scripture that picks up from where the Lord left off His reading of Isaiah as recorded in Luke 4. Jesus read that Scripture in the synagogue after He returned home from His baptism by water through John and then by fire through Holy Spirit in the wilderness.

CHAPTER 3

The Scroll I Have Been Given—For the Display of His Splendor

I ASKED THE LORD RECENTLY WHAT WAS THE SPECIFIC message that He wanted me to preach and to watch over. He took me to the Book of Revelation. In those Scriptures, John was given a scroll that contained the things that He had seen. There was a season He was supposed to hold those things secret, and then there was a season of release. On the pages that follow is the scroll that I have been given. They contain the things that the Lord has shown me, those Jeremiah 33:3 great and mighty things, and they contain the places He has sent me. This scroll is tied to some very distinctive things—to my love of history and to my love of cities. It is tied to my specific call to root up and plant; it is tied to my redeemed life, and even to the date and place of my birth. It is tied to my prophetic giftings: to see and then declare and steward (watch over) what I have seen. It is tied to my anointing to rally the troops, both angelic hosts and people He has simply called "my family."

And this scroll is rooted in the revelation of God's love, His character, and His ways that He has expressed in His covenants with Abraham, Moses, David and Jesus. This scroll reveals the intricacies of God's covenantal faithfulness, and the elaborate measures He takes to bring us into His plans for a fruitful, triumphant, and eternal life with Him. It is tied to my desire as a little girl to be able to preach the gospel to bring about change. It is the change that Jesus actually brought. It is a change that transformed lives, and then, through the apostles and disciples, transformed cities and nations. Jesus' death, resurrection by the Spirit, and His sending forth Holy Spirit to His disciples laid the groundwork for this multiplication of His transformational impact. The Scripture in Isaiah 61 that was living then, is still living now by His Spirit; and it is the set time for it to unfold. That Scripture is the promise of my scroll: "**They will rebuild the ancient ruins and restore the places long devastated; they will renew the ruined cities that have been devastated for generations.**" (Isaiah 61:4, NIV).

Take and eat—for this scroll is tied to harvest and to the next great awakening, which is upon us now!

PART TWO:

The Root of Covenant

CHAPTER 4

Covenant—An Overview

A COVENANT IS A CONTRACT BETWEEN TWO PARTIES. More accurately per several bible scholars, it is a one-sided grant given by God, which may be conditional or unconditional. First and foremost, all Scripture is God-breathed and useful for equipping (2 Timothy 3:16). However, I have learned that I can often gain a deeper perspective on any given matter by looking at it in Scripture from the lens of both Genesis and Revelation, plus what Jesus may have said about it, what Holy Spirit is saying about it, and what teaching on it is coming through those the Lord has me aligned with.

The covenants of God are at the core of both the Old and New Testaments, particularly the eternal covenant made with Abraham. The Abrahamic covenant is one that God initiated and one that He still defends. It required His supernatural intervention to even bring about the promises made. When God called Abram, he was already 75, and he and his wife Sarai did not yet have any children. The promise contained descendants that could not be numbered as well as a land already occupied by other people.

Genesis 12: 2-3 (NIV): "I will make you into a great nation, and I will bless you; I will make your name great, and you will be a blessing. I will bless those who bless you, and whoever curses you I will curse; and all peoples on earth will be blessed through you."

In Genesis 15:1, 12-20 (NIV), we see the Lord's Covenant with Abram was reconfirmed to him in a vision and then made through blood sacrifice, and it was given a timeframe for it to manifest — when the iniquity of the Amorites would reach its fullness: After this, the word of the LORD came to Abram in a vision … As the sun was setting, Abram fell into a deep sleep, and a thick and dreadful darkness came over him. Then the LORD said to him, "Know for certain that for four hundred years your descendants will be strangers in a country not their own and that they will be enslaved and mistreated there. But I will punish the nation they serve as slaves, and afterward they will come out with great possessions. You, however, will go to your ancestors in peace and be buried at a good old age. In the fourth generation your descendants will come back here, for the sin of the Amorites has not yet reached its full measure." When the sun had set and darkness had fallen, a smoking firepot with a blazing torch appeared and passed between the pieces. On that day the LORD made a covenant with Abram and said, "To your descendants I give this land, from the Wadi of Egypt to the great river, the Euphrates—the land of the Kenites, Kenizzites, Kadmonites, Hittites, Perizzites, Rephaites, Amorites, Canaanites, Girgashites and Jebusites."

In Genesis 17:3-8 (NIV), we see the covenant being extended through Abraham to the nations:

Abram fell facedown, and God said to him, "As for me, this is my covenant with you: You will be the father of many nations. No longer will you be called Abram; your name will be Abraham, for I have made you a father of many nations. I will make you very fruitful; I will make nations of you, and kings will come from you. I will establish my covenant as an everlasting covenant between me and you and your descendants after you for the generations to come, to be your God and the God of your descendants after you. The whole land of Canaan, where you now reside as a foreigner, I will give as an everlasting possession to you and your descendants after you; and I will be their God."

Genesis 18:19 (NIV), For I have chosen him, so that he will direct his children and his household after him to keep the way of the LORD by doing what is right and just, so that the LORD will bring about for Abraham what he has promised him.

The covenant was to flow through Abraham and Sarah via their son Isaac. However along the way, Sarai considered her body unfruitful; thus, she gave her handmaiden to Abram, and in this way Ishmael was conceived and born. But, Ishmael was not the son of promise and even had to be sent away. God still blessed Ishmael and made him a great nation. It was after a visitation from the LORD wherein the LORD prophesied to Abraham and Sarah, "I will surely return to you about this time next year. Your wife Sarah will have a son" Genesis 18:10b (NIV), that Isaac was conceived and born. When it was time for Isaac to take a wife, Abraham sent his servant out to find one from their people and the servant was led to Rebekah. Isaac and Rebekah had twins Esau and Jacob; Esau was born first but Jacob was the one who received the blessing. Jacob had twelve sons and along the way, his name was changed to Israel. (I believe there are dynamics of the Isaiah 19 highway prophecy concerning Egypt, Assyria and Israel that are rooted in that clarified covenant detailed in Genesis 17 as Abraham had other children — Ishmael, Esau and children by Keturah after Sarah died, and the Israelites intermarried while in captivity in both Egypt and Babylon.)

So, God found Abram, a man who at the time was childless, as one who would teach His children. Therefore, the Lord walked with this family. He walked with them through their mistakes, and He blessed them for their acts of faith. Abraham and Sarah ended well and are listed in the Hall of Faith found in the Book of Hebrews.

CHAPTER 5

400 years of slavery prophecy fulfilled

JACOB, OR ISRAEL, FAVORED HIS SON JOSEPH AND GAVE him a coat of many colors, which essentially meant that he did not labor in the fields like his brothers. Joseph had a dream and told his brothers about it, and they decided to kill him because of it, but instead sold him into slavery. Joseph went through his journey of being placed in a pit, serving at an Egyptian's home as a slave, being falsely accused and imprisoned until through his prophetic gift of dream interpretation, he became second in command in Egypt. The Lord further blessed Joseph with wisdom and gave him the strategy of the storehouses to save Egypt from an impending famine. Many came to Egypt when the famine struck as Egypt had the needed supply. Even Joseph's brothers came. As he had dreamt, they bowed down before him during their exchange. [I recently listened to a very moving teaching by Derek Prince that likened Joseph's reunion with his brothers after those 24 years of separation to what Jesus will experience when He is embraced by His brothers, the Jewish people. That revelation gave me a deeper perspective on the Scripture in Hebrews 12:2 (NIV), "For the joy set before Him, He endured the cross."]

However, there came a time thereafter, when Joseph was no longer remembered and the entire family of Israel became enslaved. After 400 years of slavery as prophesied to Abraham, there arose a deliverer in Moses. There was an edict issued around the time of Moses' birth to kill all the male Hebrew babies. Moses was saved through the actions of his sister. Many others, including perhaps Moses' older brother Aaron, were saved by the midwives who refused to follow the order. A similar edict was issued around the time of Jesus' birth. The enemy is at it again as there is a move of God on the horizon, and currently a war is raging over the ungodly abortion laws in this nation. We release a decree now for the midwives, spiritual mothers, and sisters as well as spiritual fathers and brothers to once again arise and obey God rather than man.

CHAPTER 6

The Lord establishes His first nation

THE LORD HEARD THE CRIES OF HIS PEOPLE AND called Moses into His service. Exodus 6: 2-8 (NIV): God also said to Moses, "I am the LORD. I appeared to Abraham, to Isaac and to Jacob as God Almighty, but by my name the LORD I did not make myself fully known to them. I also established my covenant with them to give them the land of Canaan, where they resided as foreigners. Moreover, I have heard the groaning of the Israelites, whom the Egyptians are enslaving, and I have remembered my covenant. Therefore, say to the Israelites: 'I am the LORD, and I will bring you out from under the yoke of the Egyptians. I will free you from being slaves to them, and I will redeem you with an outstretched arm and with mighty acts of judgment. I will take you as my own people, and I will be your God. Then you will know that I am the LORD your God, who brought you out from under the yoke of the Egyptians. And I will bring you to the land I swore with uplifted hand to give to Abraham, to Isaac and to Jacob. I will give it to you as a possession. I am the LORD.'" The name LORD is Jehovah. It means sovereign, omnipotent, and One not willing to share His glory with idols. Exodus 19:5-6 (NIV), "Now if you will obey me and keep my covenant, you will be my own special treasure from among all the peoples on earth; for all the earth belongs to me. And you will be my kingdom of priests, my holy nation. This is the message you must give to the people of Israel."

CHAPTER 7

Foreshadows

Jesus

GOD ESTABLISHED HIS SOVEREIGNTY AND DEALT with the false gods in the land first before leading them out of bondage through the blood of the Passover Lamb. This action was a foreshadowing of what Jesus was sent to do as our Passover Lamb. Jesus came to establish His kingdom and dealt with the demons, and false worship of the kingdom of this world by healing the sick, delivering people from demons, raising the dead, and addressing the religious, and political spirits of His day.

Jesus fulfilled the prophecy to Satan written in Genesis 3:15 (NIV): "And I will put enmity between you and the woman, and between your offspring and hers; he will crush your head, and you will strike his heel." The covenant with Abraham was made to provide a lineage through which Jesus could come to earth, so that this promised redemption could be fulfilled. I think about the Garden and the way it was. God freely communed with Adam there as He brought the animals to Adam for him to name. I think on how great a fall happened there with Adam and Eve's sin. I think about the slaying of a brother by a brother and the other depravity that led to the flood. I think about the great blood sacrifices that had to be made in the Tabernacle in the Wilderness, then later in the Temple, and finally Jesus' sacrifice on the cross.

I took a class about the cross several years ago. During that time, it struck me how deep the agony of God the Father (and Holy Spirit) had to be to watch the crucifixion of Jesus and to then turn His back on His beloved for even a few moments. That class examined in detail the brutality of what happened to Jesus there; I marveled about how Jesus being our Creator decided to give His body and His blood for us even before the foundation of the world. So great a love!

Galatians 3: 13-17 (NIV): Christ redeemed us from the curse of the law by becoming a curse for us, for it is written: "Cursed is everyone who is hung on a pole." He redeemed us in order that the blessing given to Abraham might come to the Gentiles through Christ Jesus, so that by faith we might receive the promise of the Spirit. Brothers and sisters, let me take an example from everyday life. Just as no one can set aside or add to a human covenant that has been duly established, so it is in this case. The promises were spoken to Abraham and to his seed. Scripture does not say "and to seeds," meaning many people, but "and to your seed," meaning one person, who is Christ. What I mean is this: The law, introduced 430 years later, does not set aside the covenant previously established by God and thus do away with the promise. For if the inheritance depends on the law, then it no longer depends on the promise; but God in his grace gave it to Abraham through a promise.

Passover is about crossing over from slavery into the Promises of God. I was particularly moved by the intricacies that the Lord went through to complete that work. We see the work of the Lord in the plagues of Egypt that dealt with their gods, and then the final one being putting the blood of the lamb on the lintels of the doorposts—in essence making a sign of the Cross—so that the Death Angel would pass over.

Passover is one of the perpetual feasts commanded by the Lord to be observed, and Jesus perfectly fulfilled the role as our Passover Lamb. Jesus was the Lamb selected, the Lamb examined, the Lamb taken to the altar, and the Lamb slain at 3 pm on that High Holy Day when the High Priest killed the Passover Lamb and cried, IT IS FINISHED. Jesus likewise cried with a loud voice IT IS FINISHED and gave up His spirit, meaning that the debt has been paid in full. We see Him called The Lamb slain in Revelation 5 as the only one worthy who can unseal the Scroll. So He is the One leading what is to come, and He has reproduced that overcoming and victorious life in us. In speaking of His death in John 12:24 (NIV), Jesus proclaims "Very truly I tell you, unless a kernel of wheat falls to the ground and dies, it remains only a single seed. But if it dies, it produces many seeds." And in Revelation 5:9b-10 (NIV), "You are worthy to take the scroll and to open its seals, because you were slain, and with your blood you purchased for God persons from every tribe and language and people and nation. You have made them to be a kingdom and priests to serve our God, and they will reign on the earth."

The Angel of God and Holy Spirit

The Angel of God can be seen in various Scriptures throughout Exodus, including the pillars of cloud and fire that were there to guide, guard, and shield the Israelites from heat and provide light. As with every great move of God, even Creation, the Spirit of God is there to hover and activate the words declared and actions taken. As the Israelites were being hemmed in by the Red Sea before them and the Egyptians pursuing them, the Lord asked Moses why he was looking to Him. He told Moses that he needed to tell the people to move on and to raise his hand and stretch out his staff (Exodus. 14:15-16). As Moses lifted up his staff, Holy Spirit as the Wind of God opened up the way for the Israelites to cross over on dry ground. Holy Spirit is there as well to instruct and to teach. The giving of the law at Mt. Sinai on the Day of Pentecost parallels the giving of Holy Spirit on that same day in Acts 2. It was a foreshadowing of the Scriptures that declared the law would be written on the hearts of men by Holy Spirit. And there were also companies of angels released that day as flames.

Jeremiah 31: 31-33 (NIV): "The days are coming," declares the LORD, "when I will make a new covenant with the people of Israel and with the people of Judah. It will not be like the covenant I made with their ancestors when I took them by the hand to lead them out of Egypt, because they broke my covenant, though I was a husband to them," declares the LORD. "This is the covenant I will make with the people of Israel after that time," declares the LORD. "I will put my law in their minds and write it on their hearts. I will be their God, and they will be my people."

Acts 2:1-4 (NIV): When the day of Pentecost came, they were all together in one place. Suddenly a sound like the blowing of a violent wind came from heaven and filled the whole house where they were sitting. They saw what seemed to be tongues of fire that separated and came to rest on each of them. All of them were filled with the Holy Spirit and began to speak in other tongues as the Spirit enabled them.

Hebrews 1:7 (NIV): In speaking of the angels he says, "He makes his angels spirits, and his servants flames of fire."

Hebrews 10:15-18 (NIV): The Holy Spirit also testifies to us about this. First he says: "This is the covenant I will make with them after that time, says the Lord. I will put my laws in their hearts, and I will write them on their minds." Then he adds: "Their sins and lawless acts I will remember no more." And where these have been forgiven, sacrifice for sin is no longer necessary.

Here and Eternity!

The Tabernacle in the Wilderness designed by God is the reality now both of our access through Christ and of eternity when God and the Lamb are forever in our midst. There are so many layers of prophetic revelation within its structure, function, and movement. Here is just a sampling:

- The Word became flesh and tabernacled with us.

- The outer linen fence representing righteousness and the badger skin over the inner court is representative of the Scriptures in Isaiah 53.

- The outer court held the brazen altar, the Cross, and the brazen laver, the Word.

- The Holy Place contained the table of shewbread—Jesus the bread of life and our sustenance; the lampstand—the seven-fold Spirit of God; and the altar of incense that had to be sprinkled with blood—representing our consecrated worship.

- The Holy of Holies housed the Ark of the Covenant containing the tablets with The Ten Commandments representing revelation, Aaron's rod that budded representing authority and the manna representing provision, which were covered by the mercy seat. The Presence of God would dwell there. The Pillar of Fire and Cloud could be visibly seen by the camp and all of Israel's enemies. Israel would move when the cloud moved and the ark of covenant would go first.

- The Israelites were encamped around the Tabernacle so it was everyone's central focus. They were in designated companies based on the tribe of their families. Judah, meaning "praise," was the tribe placed at the entryway. Psalm 100: 4 (NIV), Enter into His gates with thanksgiving, and into His courts with praise: be thankful unto Him, and bless His name.

The Tabernacle represents Jesus who came to "tabernacle with us" (John 1:14 AMPC) as well as the eternal city where the

Garden of Eden will be restored, where God and the Lamb are in the midst, the river of God flows, and the tree of Life is seemingly everywhere along that river.

Revelation 21:22-27 (NIV): I did not see a temple in the city, because the Lord God Almighty and the Lamb are its temple. The city does not need the sun or the moon to shine on it, for the glory of God gives it light, and the Lamb is its lamp. The nations will walk by its light, and the kings of the earth will bring their splendor into it. On no day will its gates ever be shut, for there will be no night there. The glory and honor of the nations will be brought into it. Nothing impure will ever enter it, nor will anyone who does what is shameful or deceitful, but only those whose names are written in the Lamb's book of life.

Revelation 22:1-5 (NIV): Then the angel showed me the river of the water of life, as clear as crystal, flowing from the throne of God and of the Lamb down the middle of the great street of the city. On each side of the river stood the tree of life, bearing twelve crops of fruit, yielding its fruit every month. And the leaves of the tree are for the healing of the nations. No longer will there be any curse. The throne of God and of the Lamb will be in the city, and his servants will serve him. They will see his face, and his name will be on their foreheads. There will be no more night. They will not need the light of a lamp or the light of the sun, for the Lord God will give them light. And they will reign for ever and ever.

Two Warnings by way of Kadesh

The Israelites sent in 12 spies to view the Promised Land. Although the land was flowing with milk and honey as the Lord had promised, there were giants in the land. Although God had delivered them and provided for them with such a great display of power, all but Joshua and Caleb chose to move in fear. The Israelites rejected the Word of the Lord, and all but Joshua and Caleb from that generation died in the wilderness. Similarly, today there are giants in our promised land, but "we are well able to take the Land" (Numbers 13:30, paraphrased). We are in a clash of kingdoms—the Kingdom of our God and the kingdom of the world. However, covenant means that God will fight for us, but we must believe.

On the second go round when the younger generation of Israelites was set to enter the Promised Land, they began to complain about the lack of water. Therefore, Moses inquired of the Lord about what to do, and he was instructed to speak to the rock. Moses in his anger, however, relied on his past method of striking the rock and even struck the rock twice. As a result, the Lord told Moses that he would not be able to enter in The Promised Land with his people. I believe this is another important lesson for us as we stand at this door of the Greatest Great Awakening. We must be led by the instructions that come from the Spirit of God versus just following what has worked in the past.

Important note about Emperor Constantine

In AD312, Emperor Constantine was in a political race. He was a worshiper of the pagan sun god Mithras. During worship, he had a vision of the cross and the sun, and he interpreted that as a message to embrace the cross. He promised to end a very heavy season of persecution and legalize Christianity. However, he had a few caveats. He wanted to make some "improvements". He abolished house churches; he then either built church structures or transitioned existing pagan temples, and he added professional choirs. He also forbade observing Passover; instead, he aligned its timing in the Spring with the pagan celebration of the fertility goddess Estra. He further changed God's calendar to be centered on the Roman gods: he added a birthday celebration for Jesus and made it the same date as Mithras' (the pagan sun god's) birthday—December 25th; and he started the week on Sunday. In addition, he changed the language of the bible to that which only a few could understand; and he forbade the reading of Scripture by the "common" people. Holy Spirit departed from this reorganized church expression, the great miracles of the early church ceased being common, and the world plummeted into the Dark Ages.

The Lord however kept lights going in the Dark Ages through the Celtic Church and a company of people called the Waldensians. And since the 1500s, the Lord through Holy Spirit has been restoring His church. Through great sacrifice of the saints, the Bible has been printed in the common language, salvation is once again by faith and not works, Holy Spirit and His gifts and authority have been recognized, and God's calendar, One New Man, and the five-fold ministry as listed in Ephesians 4 are coming to the forefront.

Ephesians 4:11-13 (NIV): So Christ himself gave the apostles, the prophets, the evangelists, the pastors and teachers, to equip his people for works of service, so that the body of Christ may be built up until we all reach unity in the faith and in the knowledge of the Son of God and become mature, attaining to the whole measure of the fullness of Christ.

CHAPTER 8

What does Covenant Look Like Today?

COVENANTS COME WITH A PROMISE, A PROPHETIC destiny, to activate and execute. God's covenants require the establishment of His Sovereignty, including a tearing down of false worship and both spiritual and practical sanctification. They also entail following His instructions and His lead, demonstrating given authority, relying on His supernatural provision, centering your daily focus on His Presence, being equipped to cultivate your giftings, living in community with your "tribe" and your "company," having faith in His vision, and being trained and ready to war for your inheritance with confidence and courage.

Because of the Blood of God's Passover Lamb, Jesus, and through accepting Jesus as Our Sovereign Lord, we have been grafted into God's eternal covenant with Abraham. Jesus' covenant however is a covenant with better promises. His covenant includes the complete annihilation of the impact of sin. It is the fulfillment of the prophecy in Jeremiah 31. His laws written on our hearts by Holy Spirit.

The Lord has given each of us seeds of a prophetic destiny, but it requires some things from us to see those seeds grow into the fulfillment of His Promise.

Mark 13:32-37 (NKJV): "But of that day and hour no one knows, not even the angels in heaven, nor the Son, but only the Father. Take heed, watch and pray; for you do not know when the time is. It is like a man going to a far country, who left his house and gave authority to his servants, and to each his work, and commanded the doorkeeper to watch. Watch therefore, for you do not know when the master of the house is coming—in the evening, at midnight, at the crowing of the rooster, or in the morning—lest, coming suddenly, he find you sleeping. And what I say to you, I say to all: Watch!"

Matthew 25:14-30 (NIV): "'Again, it will be like a man going on a journey, who called his servants and entrusted his wealth to them. To one he gave five bags of gold, to another two bags, and to another one bag, each according to his ability. Then he went on his journey. The man who had received five bags of gold went at once and put his money to work and gained five bags more. So also, the one with two bags of gold gained two more. But the man who had received one bag went off, dug a hole in the ground and hid his master's money. After a long time the master of those servants returned and settled accounts with them. The man who had received five bags of gold brought the other five. 'Master,' he said, 'you entrusted me with five bags of gold. See, I have gained five more.' His master replied, 'Well done, good and faithful servant! You have been faithful with a few things; I will put you in charge of many things. Come and share your master's happiness!' The man with two bags of gold also came. 'Master,' he said, 'you entrusted me with two bags of gold; see, I have gained two more.' His master replied, 'Well done, good and faithful servant! You have been faithful with a few things; I will put you in charge of many things. Come and share your master's happiness!' Then the man who had received one bag of gold came. 'Master,' he said, 'I knew that you are a hard man, harvesting where you have not sown and gathering where you have not scattered seed. So I was afraid and went out and hid your gold in the ground. See, here is what belongs to you.' His master replied, 'You wicked, lazy servant! So you knew that I harvest where I have not sown and gather where I have not scattered seed? Well then, you should have put my money on deposit with the bankers, so that when I returned I would have received it back with interest. So take the bag of gold from him and give it to the one who has ten bags. For whoever has will be given more, and they will have an abundance. Whoever does not have, even what they have will be taken from them. And throw that worthless servant outside, into the darkness, where there will be weeping and gnashing of teeth.'"

CHAPTER 9

A Sign Post: Modern Day Israel

I HAVE A DEEP LONGING IN MY HEART FOR MORE Christians to get a revelation of the importance of Israel. I feel that many have not grasped how much God loves His first nation, the one that He set apart and first said that He would be their God. We have not fully understood that their history shows the depth, breadth, and height of God's love, and His extreme faithfulness to His covenantal promises.

We have largely come by this disconnect because Emperor Constantine cut us off from our Jewish roots as described previously. Amongst other things, celebrating Passover was made illegal and punishable by death. There are many believers today who do not realize that Good Friday is actually Passover. For more details, I highly recommend that you read Robert Heidler's The Messianic Church Arising! book.

When Jesus came along, after 400 years of silence from the Lord, He was born into an occupied Israel. Jesus is a Jew, His first disciples and apostles were Jews, and the early church was initially composed of Messianic believers. However, Jesus was rejected by the mainstream community. That set off a cascade of events leading to the destruction of the Temple as He prophesied and the diaspora of the Jewish people and of His young church. However, the church was well-equipped and spread the gospel wherever they went with signs, wonders, and miracles following. Constantine in 312 AD slowed that, but not before Christianity literally took over the Roman Empire. However, a wave of anti-Semitism also spread.

In more recent times, some of the worst acts of inhumanity have occurred. Six million Jews were killed by various means during the Holocaust. I did not understand the depth of that horror until after my salvation. Back in 2002, I was in Washington, DC and I went to the Holocaust museum there. Then a few years later, I saw a performance in Charlotte by the International Christian Embassy Jerusalem called "The Covenant, the Story of My People," which particularly moved me as they used Scriptures out of Ezekiel 37. I could sense the Lord's heart for His people as the question was posed, "could these dry bones live?" as the cast dramatized and sang about the events that happened during the Holocaust.

The Holocaust timing ranged from January 30, 1933 – May 8, 1945; and I still stand amazed that in just three years after the last concentration camps were closed, the State of Israel was founded (May 14, 1948). The faithfulness of our God and the resilience of His people are remarkable.

From 2006-2010, I started organizing tours to Israel for the church where I belonged. When I set foot there for the first time in 2006, I felt so connected to the Land and the Lord's Presence. 2 Chronicles 7 is one of the Scriptures that describes the thickness of His glory that still rests in the Land.

2 Chronicles 7:1-3, 11-16 (NIV): When Solomon finished praying, fire came down from heaven and consumed the burnt offering and the sacrifices, and the glory of the LORD filled the temple. The priests could not enter the temple of the LORD because the glory of the LORD filled it. When all the Israelites saw the fire coming down and the glory of the LORD above the temple, they knelt on the pavement with their faces to the ground,

and they worshiped and gave thanks to the LORD, saying, "He is good; his love endures forever." ... When Solomon had finished the temple of the LORD and the royal palace, and had succeeded in carrying out all he had in mind to do in the temple of the LORD and in his own palace, the LORD appeared to him at night and said: "I have heard your prayer and have chosen this place for myself as a temple for sacrifices. When I shut up the heavens so that there is no rain, or command locusts to devour the land or send a plague among my people, if my people, who are called by my name, will humble themselves and pray and seek my face and turn from their wicked ways, then I will hear from heaven, and I will forgive their sin and will heal their land. Now my eyes will be open and my ears attentive to the prayers offered in this place. I have chosen and consecrated this temple so that my Name may be there forever. My eyes and my heart will always be there."

Some of what has most struck me:

- Israel is the keeper of The Book—how precious the Word of God is. There is Simchat Torah, a festival where they dance with the Holy Scriptures (The Torah, The Book) in the streets celebrating.

- Their government is ruled by the Word of God, the Promises of God.

- Most businesses honor the Sabbath of the Lord and there is a holy hush that falls over the Land—even the elevators are on a Sabbath timer.

- There are the young soldiers who do a mandatory service; all enter in as privates. There is a national pride that hums in the air.

- There is an honoring of family and community and connectedness because they share the same blood. It does not matter the color of their skin or the nation from which they made Aliyah (immigration to Israel).

- There is a vibrancy in the land. I remember seeing before and after pictures of what the Land looked like. There are plants being cultivated even in the dry regions and there is glory even over the wilderness places.

- There is a caring for neighbors and friends that are non-Jewish. [Leviticus 19:33-34 (AMP): "When a stranger resides with you in your land, you shall not do him wrong. The stranger who resides with you shall be to you as the native among you, and you shall love him as yourself, for you were aliens in the land of Egypt; I am the LORD your God."] If you look beyond the rioting, from which Israel must defend itself, you see the humanitarian aid.

- There is a sense of understanding what the kingdom of God looks like on every mountain of cultural influence. As it says in Genesis 12, "blessed to be a blessing." According to the Jewish Virtual Library, between 1901 and 2018, at least 203 of the more than 900 Nobel Prize winners have been Jewish. According to an opinion column entitled "The Tel Aviv Cluster" written by David Brooks in January 2010 (as published in the New York Times), Jews make up 0.2 percent of the world population, but 54 percent of the world chess champions, 27 percent of the Nobel physics laureates, and 31 percent of the medicine laureates. And in the U.S., Jews make up 2 percent of the population, but 21 percent of the Ivy League student bodies, 26 percent of the Kennedy Center honorees, 37 percent of the Academy

Award-winning directors, 38 percent of those on a recent Business Week list of leading philanthropists, and 51 percent of the Pulitzer Prize winners for nonfiction. He also noted that there are several Jewish names leading hi-tech companies such as: Intel (Grove and Vadasz), Google (Brin and Page), Oracle (Ellison), Microsoft (Balmer), Dell (Dell), and Facebook (Zuckerberg and Sandberg). And generally, some of the noted names for significant achievements throughout modern history who happen to be Jewish include:

- o Albert Einstein, theoretical physicist who developed the theory of relativity.

- o Dr. Jonas Salk created the first polio vaccine.

- o Dr. Abraham Waksman coined the term antibiotics.

- o Casmir Funk, a Polish Jew, pioneered a new field of medical research and coined the word "vitamins."

- o Dr. Paul "Magic Bullet" Ehrlich won the Nobel Prize in 1908 for curing syphilis.

- o Dr. Abraham Jacobi is considered America's father of pediatrics.

- o Haym Solomon and Isaac Moses are responsible for creating the first modern banking institutions.

- o Jews created the first department stores including: B. Altman & Co. (1865-1990), Gimbels (1887-1987), Kaufmanns (1871-2006), Mays

(1877-2005), and Abraham & Straus, later A&S, (1865-1995.

o Samuel L. Goldwyn and Louis B. Mayer (MGM) produced the first full-length sound picture, *The Jazz Singer*.

o European Jews are the founding fathers of all the Hollywood Studios.

o Irving Berlin and George and Ira Gershwin are three of the most prolific composers of the 20th century.

o Theodor Judah was chief architect and engineer for the American Transcontinental railroad.

o Marc Chagall (born Segal, Russia) is one of the greatest painters of the 20th century.

o The famous poem of Jewish Poet Emma Lazarus—"give me your tired ... your poor ... your huddled masses ..."—appears as the inscription on the Statue of Liberty.

Looking at Israel and the accomplishment of the Jewish people has given me a new sense of respect for the covenant into which we have been grafted. There is a deeper understanding of Romans 9:4-5 and 11:11-12 (NIV): …to whom pertain the adoption, the glory, the covenants, the giving of the law, the service of God, and the promises; of whom are the fathers and from whom, according to the flesh, Christ came, who is over all, the eternally blessed God. Amen…. Again I ask: Did they stumble so as to fall beyond recovery? Not at all! Rather, because of their transgression, salvation has come to the Gentiles to make Israel envious. But if their transgression means riches for the world, and their loss means riches for the Gentiles, how much greater riches will their full inclusion bring!

We are in a historic moment in time. We have just passed in 2018, Israel's 70th Anniversary of her Regathering into the Land. The United States was the first nation to recognize Israel's statehood in 1948 under President Truman, and now the first nation to have its embassy in Jerusalem under President Trump. I was blessed to visit the Land once more in 2018 to honor their historic anniversary. At least two of our guides, as they recalled their history, remarked that through all the various invasions —"we are still here" and "no other culture has kept their language, their traditions" through a dispersion like they had experienced.

CHAPTER 10

What does this Root of Covenant mean for a Christian believer?

WE HAVE BEEN GRAFTED INTO THE ROOT OF GOD'S covenant with Abraham. We need to recognize the strength of the authority our relationship with Christ has brought us. We need to recognize the fullness of who our Sovereign God is and the power that resides in His promises, in Holy Spirit, and the holy angels. Just as it was promised to Abraham that he would be a father of many nations (Genesis 17:4 NIV), Jesus, the Seed of Abraham, is the Desire of All Nations (Haggai 2:7). Psalm 2 speaks of His inheritance in the nations. And, throughout the Book of Revelation—such as in chapter 7 verse 9 (NIV), we see "a great multitude that no one could count, from every nation, tribe, people and language, standing before the throne and before the Lamb."

A Testimony—Where is my Inheritance?

It was October 2013; my grandfather had recently passed away. Grandpop was 98 at his passing and my last parental figure. Both my parents had gone home to be with the Lord – my dad in 2002 and my mom in 2006. It had been difficult trying to take care of Grandpop since dementia was setting in and my mom had already passed. My sister once again bore the weight of his care-giving as she lived in Pennsylvania only a couple of hours away from him, while I lived nine hours away in North Carolina.

I was at home grieving, feeling alone and abandoned. So I started talking, or rather complaining, to the Lord about some of the difficulties with extended family members that my sister in reality had to face. I was really crying out to the Lord about all of that. I was like, "Lord, where is our inheritance that you prom-ised?" And I went on to ask Him as I was of African descent, "Lord, where do we even come from?" I was really going at it as I felt orphaned, so to speak, even though I was already over 50 years old.

In those very moments, I felt the Lord sweep me up and place me back in the Garden of Eden. It was like we were standing together there. It seemed that I was somehow in an elevated place where I could also see beyond the garden. I saw His arm extend out, His finger pointing out, and then I heard Genesis 1:28: "Be fruitful and multiply, fill the earth, and subdue it." (NIV) "Aahhh, I see," I responded … "the earth is yours; I am yours; so the earth is mine."

We are co-heirs with Christ, co-laborers in His kingdom, and we are called to steward the earth. So, my Abba, the all-pow-erful God, the One who made all things, also stops to draw one to Himself who is hurting. He stops to comfort and bring peace. He makes Himself so real that every storm is quieted. He hears our prayers, knows our thoughts, and He cares. He watches over His Word to perform it.

Psalm 2:8 (NIV): "Ask of me, and I will make the nations your inheritance, the ends of the earth your possession."

Acts 1:8 (NIV): "But you will receive power when the Holy Spirit comes on you; and you will be my witnesses in Jerusalem, and in all Judea and Samaria, and to the ends of the earth."

Galatians 3:8 (NIV): "The Scripture foresaw that God would justify the Gentiles by faith, and announced the gospel in advance to Abraham: 'All nations will be blessed through you.'"

Ephesians 2: 13-22 (NIV): But now in Christ Jesus you who once were far away have been brought near by the blood of Christ. For he himself is our peace, who has made the two groups one and has destroyed the barrier, the dividing wall of hostility, by setting aside in his flesh the law with its commands and regulations. His purpose was to create in himself one new humanity out of the two, thus making peace, and in one body to reconcile both of them to God through the cross, by which he put to death their hostility. He came and preached peace to you who were far away and peace to those who were near. For through him we both have access to the Father by one Spirit. Consequently, you are no longer foreigners and strangers, but fellow citizens with God's people and also members of his household, built on the foundation of the apostles and prophets, with Christ Jesus himself as the chief cornerstone. In him the whole building is joined together and rises to become a holy temple in the Lord. And in him you too are being built together to become a dwelling in which God lives by his Spirit.

A Testimony—The People of my dreams

In the months that followed this encounter I saw a demonstration of what the Lord is doing in the nations. When I was a young believer, I had an extended season of vivid dreams of visiting various people groups, including those living on the Pacific islands, South America, Vietnam, Korea, and then some people that I could not identify. The Lord confirmed these dreams with prophecies received over the years, and He has indeed blessed me to "go to the nations," including Ghana, England, Canada, Israel, Korea, Haiti, Italy, Germany, and France.

In December 2013, I somehow came across a series of interviews with Terry Law by Rick Joyner. It was Terry Law's book

The Power of Praise and Worship that helped me understand the night vision I had in January 1990 (which I describe in detail in the next section). Since reading his book over 25 years ago, I had not heard anything further about Terry Law. Those interviews in 2013 described the critical work that Terry and his team did in Poland behind the Iron Curtain in the 70s and 80s through worship and praise. I believe his ministry there played a key role in the Iron Curtain coming down, an event I never believed I would see happen in my lifetime. While growing up through until I was 30, Communism was a dark cloud draping more than half of the world's population.

In the last interview with Rick, Terry made an appeal for folks to turn their hearts towards the Middle East as that is the "Iron Curtain" of this day and to consider going to Kurdistan, a nation that is open to Christians, and to Israel. Something within me resonated deeply, so I looked up the Kurds and, aha, my eyes fell on some of the previously unidentified people in my dreams.

In July 2015, the Lord began to connect the dots. My close friend and Releasing Heaven Ministries teammate Becky and I made a chance visit to see some friends in Nashville. Although we kept in touch somewhat via Facebook, I had not been to Nashville to visit our friends in ten years. Time flies too quickly. Two of our friends, Dawn and Joseph, graciously hosted us; and shortly after our arrival, we proceeded to make the rounds to reconnect with the others we knew there. I made a spontaneous remark during lunch with our friend Dabney about having a heart for the Kurds, and we discovered for the first time that Dabney and her husband Doug had started a work in Kurdistan in the 90s. Dabney told us that the largest population of Kurds living in the United States lived in Nashville. Then that same day we learned that Joseph had lived in Kurdistan for five years. He had even recorded a Kurdish worship CD. I immediately recognized that the Lord was up to something, so I planned a return trip to Nashville that September. On that trip, our mission team had a chance to meet Doug and

Dabney, Dawn and Joseph, plus a friend of Dabney's, Carolyn, who had lived in the Near East for nearly 15 years. Carolyn helped us pinpoint a location for our mission trip. Since the Kurdistan region is often dubbed the Cradle of Civilization, we code-named it Rivers of Glory Mission.

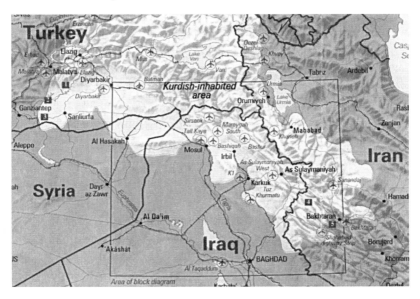

The Kurdistan region is known as modern-day Assyria. The magi who visited Jesus are believed to have come from this region. I remember in 2005-2006 having what I would call living encounters with several of the verses in Isaiah 19 which include this region; at that time, one of our scholarly friends confirmed through some Rabbinical leaders that those passages had not yet been fulfilled.

Isaiah 19:23-25 (NKJV): In that day there will be a highway from Egypt to Assyria, and the Assyrian will come into Egypt and the Egyptian into Assyria, and the Egyptians will serve with the Assyrians. In that day Israel will be one of three with Egypt and Assyria—a blessing in the midst of the land, whom the Lord of hosts shall bless, saying, "Blessed is Egypt My people, and Assyria the work of My hands, and Israel My inheritance."

One key theme that came forward during our time of preparation for our mission trip was regarding Esther and how the Lord was opening the books of remembrance just as was done when it was discovered that Mordecai had saved the king, but had not at that time been rewarded. The Lord, likewise, was rewarding the people of the region for the king having issued another decree and thereby saving the Jews. Also it is believed that it was that king's son who allowed Nehemiah to return and rebuild the wall of Jerusalem. The magi also saved Jesus by traveling back another way instead of telling Herod how to find the king whose star they had followed. We were prompted to look at our flight schedule and discovered that we just so happened to be leaving from Charlotte on the evening of the start of Purim, which is a festival about Esther's story.

During our final meeting time that Monday prior to leaving, we were able to be "sent out" with prayer like those first apostolic teams in Scripture by two of the apostolic council from Glory of Zion International—Linda Heidler and Marty Cassady. Some of the prophetic words received: "This mission is a divine calling, and you are being sent as ambassadors of the Lord, as springs and strength (Psalm 84:5-8), and also as firstfruits from Glory of Zion to the 'stan' nations. The team is being sent with angelic hosts and with the expectation of kingdom fruit with individual visitations, words, and assignments that will fit together as a corporate whole with powerful impact to the ministries, people, and territory there."

We were in-country for about a week and our assignment was to join in and add to worship and prayer. The first night there, I had a vision of Jesus walking the streets of this region with His nail pierced wrists, feet, pierced side, and striped back. The next night the worship and prayers at their service included Isaiah 53:4-5 (NIV): Surely he took up our pain and bore our suffering, yet we considered him punished by God, stricken by him, and afflicted. But he was pierced for our transgressions, he was crushed for our iniquities; the punishment that brought us peace was on him, and by his wounds we are healed.

I felt that the Lord was letting me know that He paid the price for ALL to be free. He was there in that region walking in the streets and walking on the hillside with those who were the persecutors and those who were being persecuted. The nations are His inheritance! I am by no means saying that we should not be wise with our borders; but at the same time, we must be BIG with our hearts, with our worship, with our prayers, and, as HOLY SPIRIT leads, with our FINANCES to help people come to know the One who died to set them FREE, to HEAL them, to give them LIFE, and to give them PEACE. Throughout our time there, we were hearing firsthand testimonies of dreams and visions and the manifested presence of the Lord being tangibly encountered. People ARE experiencing peace and joy AND miracles of healing and deliverance, but that is not what you would readily envision from their natural circumstance. The Lord showed me the times when He had started saying some hard things that the disciples did not understand and many fell away. He showed me how He was betrayed; and how it was in that atmosphere that He went to the cross, where He even cried out, "Father forgive them." I know that there are many who have a hard stance now against Jesus and against His disciples, but those are also the ones He went to the cross for, and this is where He is walking now. That includes people here in our cities, whose culture is completely contrary to righteousness, peace, and joy. Our cities are filled with the culture of gangs, drugs and alcohol addiction, prostitution, or simply fear, anger, and unbelief. And just as He walks amongst the nations, He is here walking. He is going after His inheritance.

Another encounter that confirms this for me happened during one of our last evenings there. During worship, I had a vision that I was able to publicly release. In the vision, I was first looking up from the ground, looking for the sun as it was break-ing through. But then, I ascended in Worship and I rose to where the Lord was. In that place, I became one with Him and my eyes became His eyes. They became as the light of the sun, shining through to everywhere I looked. The Scripture I received was from Isaiah 60:1-5a (NKJV): "Arise, shine; For your light has come! And the glory of the LORD is risen upon you. For behold, the darkness shall cover the earth, And deep darkness the people; But the LORD will arise over you, And His glory will be seen upon you. The Gentiles shall come to your light, And kings to the brightness of your rising. Lift up your eyes all around, and see: They all gather together, they come to you; Your sons shall come from afar, And your daughters shall be nursed at your side. Then you shall see and become radiant, And your heart shall swell with joy; Because the abundance of the sea shall be turned to you."

One of the brothers there responded with the Scripture out of Hebrews 12: 1-2 (NKJV): Therefore we also, since we are surrounded by so great a cloud of witnesses, let us lay aside every weight, and the sin which so easily ensnares us, and let us run with endurance the race that is set before us, looking unto Jesus, the author and finisher of our faith, who for the joy that was set before Him endured the cross, despising the shame, and has sat down at the right hand of the throne of God.

CHAPTER II

A Personal Note

THE PAGES TO FOLLOW WILL CONTAIN OTHER prophetic testimonies that show that the Lord is moving inside and outside of time. He is causing the seeds of destiny and promise that have been planted in our covenant with Him to spring forth and produce fruit. These pages testify about an assurance that the Lord's heart is for all people groups, and that there has come a fullness of time when He is once again initiating the action to fulfill His covenantal promises.

PART THREE:

Seeds of Destiny

CHAPTER 12

A Heart-Cry and a Prophetic Promise

ISAIAH 58:6-8 (NIV), "IS NOT THIS THE KIND OF FASTING I have chosen: to loose the chains of injustice and untie the cords of the yoke, to set the oppressed free and break every yoke? Is it not to share your food with the hungry and to provide the poor wanderer with shelter— when you see the naked, to clothe them, and not to turn away from your own flesh and blood? Then your light will break forth like the dawn, and your healing will quickly appear; then your righteousness will go before you, and the glory of the Lord will be your rear guard."

As I wrote in the introduction, I was a part of this amazing little storefront church in the late 80s, which was led by a pastor who believed in Holy Spirit and the power of prayer. The church was set in the midst of gangs, drugs, and poverty, but it had a vision for, and faith for, change. Our pastor was a man of action with a heart for people. He took an active part in the local community of the Full Gospel Business Men's Fellowship International (FGBMI); and he also had a solid relationship with key leaders nationally. In April 1988, when John and Anne Gimenez held their second *Washington for Jesus* rally, which was supported by FGBMI, our pastor gathered our church, and we traveled together to attend. I remember it as being cold and rainy, but we held fast.

The atmosphere there was intensely electric as we rallied with over a million other believers on the Washington Mall. We all joined together to both repent and then pray against the storms that had besieged the church in those days. The two rallies held (the first one in April 1980 which gathered 700,000 believers) were a first in those times. They were similar in concept and format to the stadium gatherings that have been springing up in recent days.

As a result of the rally our church attended, our pastor laid plans to hold a summer-long series of evangelism crusades in the community we served. He and our other church leaders mapped out the street corners and locations, and then they hired an evangelist to help us. The first couple of street crusades were poorly attended by our church members, and they yielded little fruit. At the time, I was on the worship team amongst other responsibilities. Before the next crusade, a few of us (one of the couples and I) decided to worship and pray after church. The next crusade was slated to be held in front of the crack house across from our church location. We gathered in the couple's apartment after lunch and started worshiping and praying. As we did, it felt as if I were both in their living room and also in front of this crack house. I felt the floor disappear. I was standing at the base of this tree that was growing upside down. I knew somehow that this tree was holding the people in that house captive. The people were intertwined and entangled in its branches. I instinctively reached down and grabbed ahold of all of the roots of the tree. My hand and arm had the size and strength of "another man" and I shook it with force and with authority. I shouted several times, "Let my people go!"

That afternoon, we had more of the church out for our street crusade. The people living in the house and several other neighbors were all outside. About 25 people gave their lives to the Lord that day. I remember being able to pray for several women on the steps and porch there. With tears, they repented and prayed with us, but none of them ever came inside our church. It would take several years before I connected the experience with my vision of that tree and the souls saved with the **worship and prayer** we had done. Doing worship and prayer together in the way that naturally flowed that afternoon was not typical of what our circle of friends experienced in church.

I primarily remember feeling distressed and frustrated during that summer, as at one time, I was that prodigal, and I personally knew that God could completely change the lives of the people we were encountering. Yet, I still had hope as we planned to hold our last crusade at the end of the summer in the little park across from our pastor's home. This one was going to be much larger. It was being done in conjunction with a larger, more experienced church, which had great worship. In addition, we were giving clothes away and serving food.

A Heart-Cry

The last crusade day finally arrived and things were unfolding just as planned. That little park was filled with life, love, great music, food, and giveaways; but I watched as the men who slept in that park quietly slumped back down on the park benches. I knew then that the reality of that next day would be that the people would be well fed and wearing clean clothes, but they would still be in despair, without transformation, and without hope. I thought about the woman at the well in Scripture who was sneaking out to get water in order to avoid the other women because of the sinful life she was living. I thought about how Jesus had purposely set things up so that He could talk with her. He even revealed to her who He was. After just that one encounter, that one conversation, she believed and unashamedly ran to tell the whole town how she had met a man who knew everything about her. I also thought about the many challenges I had faced in my journey with others who did not believe. I began to wonder how we could overcome unbelief if there was no demonstration of power. So I stepped outside of the park that day, stood on the sidewalk, turned my face upward, and cried out to the Lord in heart-wrenching agony, "Where is Your power Lord that I read about in Your Word?"

I know my fire, my zeal began to wane a bit that day. Without the fire, the troubles that I saw both inside and outside the church began to weigh on me. Hope deferred truly does make the heart sick. It was not until January 1990 that I realized the Lord had already begun to set things in motion for the depth of transformation I longed to see in people's lives and in our cities. Actually, our being able to catch His vision and that of our Heavenly Father's was and is His prayer. It is the essence of how He taught us we should pray. Matthew 6:9-10 (NIV) reads, "This, then, is how you should pray: 'Our Father in heaven, hallowed be your name, your kingdom come, your will be done, on earth as it is in heaven.'"

A Prophetic Promise—A Night Vision

A year and a half after my passionate prayer to the Lord to see transformation in my city, I got a job offer with a company located in Phillipsburg, New Jersey. I had never lived that far away before. While in college, I lived on campus at the University of Pennsylvania, which was located right in West Philadelphia; and then I lived in Chester, Pennsylvania, which was only 20 minutes from Philadelphia's city limits. I checked with my pastor about the new job, because taking it would mean that I would have to leave the church. To my dismay, all signals were go. Therefore, I accepted the job, rented out my house, and found an apartment in Bethlehem, Pennsylvania which was just across the river from Phillipsburg. Then in January 1990, the company-scheduled movers came to get all of my possessions; and in just a few hours, I was unloaded in my new place, feeling quite a bit exiled, and very alone.

On that first night there, I had a very vivid night vision. In this vision, I was part of a small advance team that had come into a small town or village. It felt like we were just two or three in number. We went about praying over the land and looking for people to pray for; but there was just a darkness, a sadness over the land and over the people. Our prayers seemed not to have any impact at all. As we made our way through the town, we saw the rest of our team arrive. The full team quickly went over to this restaurant-bar and began to set up their musical instruments. Then, for what seemed like hours, we all joined in together for a combination of worship and spiritual warfare. When we finished and went outside, the atmosphere of the town had completely changed. It was bright and clear, and there seemed to be a hum of life and joy; and a flood of healing miracles followed.

I asked, "Lord, what was that? Where is that? How do I get to do that?" I had never seen worship and prayer flow together like that before. It looked like the Lord was saying, "That is what will bring the power for breakthrough." I pondered these things and waited with my eyes wide open in expectancy.

CHAPTER 13

The Waiting—The Lord's Training Plan

WHEN THE LORD GIVES A PROMISE, HE ALREADY HAS a plan. He trains our hands for war.

As I waited and looked for what I had seen in my vision, I came across a book by Terry Law called <u>The Power of Praise and Worship</u>. Terry talked about the power of our own words and the power of the spoken Word of God. He also gave teaching and illustrations about sacrificing praise, and about how the Word of God is magnified with praise: faith increases and power and authority increase. He taught how God Himself is enthroned on our praise, how our relationship with Him becomes more intimate, and how God uses praise as a weapon against our enemy. All of these points were Scripturally-based and known to me, but Terry's testimonies made the Word come alive in new ways. Again, I pondered these things in my heart.

I got busy looking for a new church home and became a bit frustrated in my search as weeks passed. On a visit to see my parents, I made a seemingly chance visit to the church that had helped with the outreach in front of my former pastor's house. The worship at this church had the fire of what I read about in Terry Law's book. I saw outreach at an entirely new level there. Both economic development and discipleship were blossoming as folks involved in gangs and illicit activities were coming to the Lord in what felt like droves. This church purchased and renovated one of the entertainment venues in the middle of North Philadelphia. And even my two choir buddies from college days were in leadership there. I was so excited to see what I had been looking for. During this season, I traveled to the church on the weekends, but I wanted to participate more. Therefore, I moved back to the city and tried to commute to work. After about five months and a couple of near-misses with an early morning trucker, I left that job and waited. One day as I drove past my alma mater, I heard the Lord ask if I wanted to work there. I immediately said yes and began the process of applying. I received several discouraging words of advice, but I held firm. In the meantime, I served the church where needed, first as an usher, then I added volunteering as a production assistant for one of the members' musical production (many people from the community got saved during the performances), and later I volunteered as an assistant to the church administrator. The job I applied for at my alma mater came through, and the Lord proved to me that He provides when you follow His instructions —although my money on-hand and at the bank dwindled down to pennies, I never missed a car or rent payment.

Then the enemy came. Although several of us in the church prayed, individually and in teams, our pastor did not want to hold corporate prayer meetings. In what felt like a sudden shift, everything changed—the church split and was eventually dismantled. It was a very painful season, but the Lord was faithful and much fruit has blossomed since then from many who served there. Several now have their own churches or are ministry leaders, and several others are successful business leaders.

At the height of its effectiveness, I witnessed in this church the importance of being a family (having spiritual mothers, fathers, and siblings for love, support, and correction) and the importance of collaborating as a community (using and supporting gifts, talents, and abilities) in rebuilding lives. I saw the transformational power of equipping believers in the other mountains of influence, such as the arts, media, and business, which is the more complete mandate called out in Ephesians 4.

Over the years, I have looked back over my walk with the Lord and reflected on the key visions and prophecies given. From this portion of my journey, in addition to the positive lessons learned, I gathered that corporate prayer was an essential component of lasting change.

Ghana Then Tulsa Then Back Again

The Lord in His grace continued on with His training plan by having me answer a call to go on my first mission trip. In this season, the Lord had spoken to me about my call to preach and my call as a prophet. I figured that must mean that I needed to go to bible school. I was looking for one locally when I started receiving information from the minister leading the mission trip about the bible school in Tulsa, Oklahoma, where she lived. Consequently, I made plans to move to Oklahoma to attend bible school after the mission trip.

The mission trip was both hard and glorious. It brought me to the nation of Ghana, which, I found out only recently, is a key part of my ancestral history. The trip also put me in several of the churches planted by one of the key leaders in that region, Archbishop Benson Idahosa. I remember feeling so empowered when I read his biography, Fire in His Bones, while I was still living in Bethlehem. I witnessed a number of miracles similar to those he described during my six-week mission assignment; I was even healed of endometriosis. Moreover, our hosts took us to the caves where my ancestors were probably sold, and the team of Ghanaians who accompanied us repented with great sorrow and tears for selling us into slavery. I also witnessed the power outages and sanitation problems, and I wondered why America was so blessed. Here were spirit-filled believers, who loved the Lord and loved their nation, and they were highly educated; but yet, there would be outbreaks of disease and obvious signs of witchcraft being actively practiced. A thought to ponder.

Once back stateside, I found out that bible school was not a viable option for me. Therefore, I spent the remainder of my year and a half in Oklahoma in great despair. By the time I moved back to Pennsylvania, I had nothing but my clothes and my car. I had sold my house and had given away most of my possessions. I was heavily complaining until one night about 3:00 am, I felt this hard tap, or rather slap, on my shoulder. When I woke up, there was an angel in my room. I could not tell whether the angel was male or female but "she" looked Asian. She was wearing what looked like a Chinese officer's military uniform. I quickly hit the deck and repented for my attitude. I had a couple of other encounters with angels prior to that night, but I immediately knew that there was now a shift—I was now in the Army of the Lord.

I returned to Pennsylvania in 1995. First I stayed at my sister's home in central Pennsylvania, but after six months, I ventured back to Philadelphia. I spent a good season living on a friend's couch before I found a job and was able to rent my own apartment. Strangely though, Philadelphia no longer felt like home. I began having dreams of tall trees and different styles of homes. So in 1997, I found myself driving a moving truck with my few possessions to Charlotte, NC. Almost immediately, I came upon a Friday Night Watch with worship and spiritual warfare being used together. Eureka!

The Carolinas

For the next 11 years, I experienced the dynamics that I remembered reading about in Terry Law's book. My prophetic gifting increased as I was given opportunity to minister on prayer, prophetic, and ministry teams. One of my first memories was feeling the presence of an angel standing in front of me as I stood in the prayer line. I felt him put on me what felt like one of those lead chest coverings used in dental offices when they take x-rays. I was quietly asking the Lord what that was when the prophetic word came forth saying that there were angels present in the room who were either repairing or replacing our armor. I was one that was having a replacement done, for sure. There were very powerful prophetic words released during those Watch times and often team members would have dreams during the week and bring those forward as well. The prophetic revelation at times ranged from praying for a military pilot who was discerned to be in trouble, to a school where a terrorist attack had been planned and executed, to things that were happening in our own city and region, and to very personal words of encouragement and comfort. It was such an honor to serve amongst a company of people with these gifts and to see God answer prayers.

I also served there practically. My responsibilities ranged from helping with the overheads (before we had projection screens), to serving and then leading the youth group, to serving and then leading the Sound Department, to being a home group leader, to helping form and run a bible college, to being a Watch leader and leader of various other ministry teams, and to planning our team ministry trips, women's retreats, Israel tours, and more. We did not have an active Outreach to the community until I was assigned that responsibility as a part of our bible college program.

These were very powerful times. I learned much about prayer, including how to be a good steward of both my personal and corporate prayer life. I was blessed to serve in so many different capacities. All along the way, the Lord was keeping that vision I had in 1990 alive.

One of the prophetic things I saw that encouraged me was seeing, while praying in 2002, what I call "glory balls" hitting about 20 key cities in the United States. Chuck Pierce and Dutch Sheets visited 23 cities in the 2017-2018 time period; they will be visiting 20 or so cities in 2019-2020 to gather the Army of the Lord regionally to plow for the next Awakening. In the next part of this book, "this scroll," I share about their visits to our region as those visits hold significance for the nation. And as I am putting the final touches on this book, Glory of Zion just held its Passover 5779 Conference, wherein Dutch released a dream about standing on an ancient path with the key to an open heaven. And Chuck prophesied about seven cylinders of fiery arrows coming down through that open heaven and about the rallying of the troops to release those fiery arrows that would penetrate the earth to reconnect the land to covenantal triumph. And from another source, I also recently heard that plans are underway within different organizations for the hosting of stadium worship gatherings in about 20 cities across the United States that may all just so happen to coincide on the same date in 2020. *Yes Lord, release your fire and your rain!*

In 2004, I had a prophetic vision of a herd of wild horses of various breeds running fast and free across the plains of Texas towards the East Coast. In my spirit, I knew that somehow one of the sparks for the Awakening I had been waiting for would come out of Texas. I am not surprised that the ministry the Lord eventually aligned me with is based in Corinth, Texas. And there now are a number of powerful global ministries based in that same region.

Another key thing that encouraged me along the way was the Lord's discipline—following His ways, thinking about and doing what He would do. I was recently reflecting with a friend about the importance of serving others, including extending yourself to your neighbor. Being a good neighbor was even one of the major themes of a recent city-wide gathering of churches, ministries, non-profits, government, and business leaders. Also, during one of our recent weather emergencies, for the first time ever that I can recall, I heard City officials say, "Check on your neighbors as your first response since we will not be able to get to everyone in a timely fashion." This friend and I were both reflecting about how life without Jesus would be so empty, and how nothing other than Him can really satisfy. She began speaking about the way Luke 10:27-28 reads in one translation—that it says how loving Him and loving our neighbor is **to have life**. I found that Complete Jewish Bible translation and it does read that way – wow! Starting at verse 25, it reads: An expert in Torah stood up to try and trap him by asking, "Rabbi, what should I do to obtain eternal life?" But Yeshua said to him, "What is written in the Torah? How do you read it?" He answered, "You are to love Adonai your God with all your heart, with all your soul, with all your strength and with all your understanding; and your neighbor as yourself." "That's the right answer," Yeshua said. "Do this, and **you will have life.**"

I remember sharing about two years ago with my Releasing Heaven Ministries family about why I give so much. It is because I have been forgiven of much, and because I have discovered that the Lord is good. He is My Salvation, My Help, My Confidant, My Healer, My Provider, My Deliverer, and recently He told me that He is My Defender. I consider myself an athlete when it comes to the things of the Lord. I discipline myself; I cultivate my spiritual life; and I practically put the Lord first, with my time, my thought process, and my other relationships, whether with family or friends. I found some of my notes from a bible study teaching that I gave. There are several Scriptures that jump out at me even now. Hebrews 11:6 (ESV), "And without faith it is impossible to please him, for whoever would draw near to God must believe that he exists and that he rewards those who seek him." We have to believe in His Goodness to choose to draw near to Him. It often takes fire, trials, to know that He is good. God allowed the Egyptians to chase down the Israelites so that both the Egyptians and the Israelites would know Him. As you can see in some of my missteps, our attitude while we go through trials and tribulations makes a HUGE difference. Colossians 3:23-24 (ESV), "Whatever you do, work heartily, as for the Lord and not for men, knowing that from the Lord you will receive the inheritance as your reward. You are serving the Lord Christ." 2 Timothy 2:5 (ESV), "An athlete is not crowned unless he competes according to the rules."

I know there are those in the body of Christ who are just biding time until Jesus returns. They are looking forward to that day when there are no more tears, no more pain, no more sorrow. Truly, that day will be glorious when we can live with Jesus FOREVER, where He is our light, where the River of God FREELY flows, and where the very streets are made of gold. In the testimonies of those who have visited heaven, I have heard that there is so much color there, and the trees, grass, and flowers are singing. I too long for THAT day! *BUT, let us not meet Him empty-handed.*

CHAPTER 14

The Sprouting—The Dew

Israel

IN 2006, I WAS ABLE TO TAKE MY VERY FIRST TRIP TO Israel. As I mentioned in the chapters on The Root of Covenant, there is a profound sense of the Lord's Presence there. There is such an honor of God there—an honor of His Word, honor of His Holiness exhibited in how they worship and pray at the Western Wall and in the tunnels running underneath the wall, and honor of His faithfulness, knowing that they are His chosen people. He has proven it. There is a sense of understanding what the kingdom of God looks like on every mountain of cultural influence. There is an understanding of family and community based on shared history and shared blood. There is a maturing that seems to happen. It is a true blessing that comes when you bless God's first nation. I believe in my heart that to honor the Lord's first nation and to obey His commands concerning her has thrust me forward in my destiny. I also believe that the fulfillment of the prophecies in Ezekiel and other Scriptures, with Israel being back in her land and having rule over Jerusalem has hastened the day of Awakening that is upon us.

Azusa

Also in 2006, the Lord quickened me to attend the 100th year Anniversary celebration of the Azusa Street Revival in Los Angeles. It was an electrifying time even to wait outside in the crowds to gain entrance. There were so many people there from all over the world. It was such a thrill to see such hunger for the Glory of the Lord. It is always good to know that there are others who feel as deeply and as passionately about the Lord as I do. During the years of helping to lead the bible college, I took a deeper dive into the history of the Revivals and Awakenings of the past. Since then, I have come across Tommy Welchel's books about the miracles even the children of Azusa Street saw and experienced. The children witnessed limbs being grown out, eyeballs forming where there had been none, growths and tumors falling off, the lame walking, the deaf and dumb hearing and rejoicing, and everyone encountering the Lord's thick Presence. The supernatural flames of this revival could be physically seen— fire trucks had been called out on occasion.

At its height, this revival was led by a one-eyed, African American pastor named William Seymour. The revival was attended by all races. Papa Seymour (as he was affectionately known) had been trained and mentored by Charles Fox Parham. Parham's message was that modern Christians could receive the baptism in Holy Spirit with the evidence of speaking in tongues, as did the first apostles. (It was in Parham's bible school in Topeka, Kansas in 1901 that a student named Agnes Ozman was the first to speak in tongues.) It has been reported that the movement that started at Azusa Street is at the root of every Pentecostal movement ever since. The movement spread in the 60s through the Protestant churches, and then into the Roman Catholic Church. The estimated impact has been 600 million.

Virginia Beach—Pre-Appointed Times & Boundaries

In September 2007, I was prompted by the Lord to attend a conference in Virginia Beach. I had arrived early. I was getting ready to walk the beach with a friend when a pastor stopped to tell us about Rev. Robert Hunt. He asked us if we knew how close we were to the First Landing. Even though I had been taking a deep dive on Revival History, I did not recall ever hearing about Robert Hunt or the First Landing. With modern technology being as it is, I continued my walk while I looked up who Rev. Robert Hunt was and exactly what was the First Landing.

I discovered that Rev. Hunt was an Anglican minister who was commissioned under the Virginia Charter to evangelize the land that stretched from South Carolina to Maine and far to the west. The location was called the First Landing because it was the place that the permanent colony of Jamestown had first come onto the shores of this land. Rev. Hunt carried a huge wooden cross with him. After first making the crew stay on board for three days of fasting and praying, he led them ashore on April 29, 1607. They immediately dedicated this land to the Lord.

Rev. Hunt's prayer: "We do hereby dedicate this Land, and ourselves, to reach the People within these shores with the Gospel of Jesus Christ, and to raise up Godly generations after us, and with these generations take the Kingdom of God to all the earth. May this Covenant of Dedication remain to all generations, as long as this earth remains, and may this Land, along with England, be Evangelist to the World. May all who see this Cross, remember what we have done here, and may those who come here to inhabit join us in this Covenant and in this most noble work that the Holy Scriptures may be fulfilled" It is reported that Rev. Hunt then used covenantal language to declare, "From these very shores the Gospel shall go forth not only to this New World but the entire world." At the end of the prayer, he read a passage from Psalm 22:27-28 (KJV), "All the ends of the world shall remember and turn to the Lord, and all the kindreds of the nations shall worship before thee. For the kingdom is the Lord's and he ruleth among the nations."

I read that Rev. Hunt was married with children, and that he did not survive beyond the following year, dying at age 39. I felt a kindred connection with him, as I already was past that age, and marveled at the great risk he took to travel to a land that had yet to see a colony survive. I knew it had to be the Lord who drew him. I thought about another man, Dr. King, who similarly had a call of God on his life, which he pursued even though the risk was great and the likelihood strong that he would not personally survive. I have found that many of us miss the last part of the verse when we quote Revelation 12:10-11 (NASB), but neither Rev. Hunt or Dr. King missed it: "Then I heard a loud voice in heaven, saying, 'Now the salvation, and the power, and the kingdom of our God and the authority of His Christ have come, for the accuser of our brethren has been thrown down, he who accuses them before our God day and night. And they overcame him because of the blood of the Lamb and because of the word of their testimony, and they did not love their life even when faced with death.'"

As the Virginia Beach conference progressed, my spirit was stirred about Acts 17:26-27 (NKJV): "And He has made from one blood every nation of men to dwell on all the face of the earth, and has determined their pre-appointed times and the boundaries of their dwellings, so that they should seek the Lord, in the hope that they might grope for Him and find Him, though He is not far from each one of us." Suddenly, I could feel the Lord's heart for this nation. I knew in those moments that it did not matter how I got here, but that I was planted in this nation on purpose, for such a time as this. Immediately my love for this nation and for her call deepened. I thought about the fact that I was born on Flag Day in Philadelphia, the City of Brotherly Love. I remembered a class I took in college called "Black Lawyers and Social Change." I remembered how those lawyers risked their lives to strategize about how to effect change, at least in the legal system. I thought about the people engaged in those court cases centered on desegregating the public schools, and how it was apparent that God had purposely planted people with courage to be the answer in their generation. I believe that we are all called to be an answer. The questions remain: whom and what will we believe? The Lord has great promises. There are always giants in the land. So, will we follow the path of Joshua and Caleb, Linda Brown and her dad Oliver who were the plaintiffs in the Brown versus Board of Education of Topeka, Kansas court case, Dr. King, and Rev. Hunt, or will we fall victim to the taunts of the naysayers, the Goliaths and their kindred? (An interesting side note is that the spark of Awakening with Agnes Ozman in 1901 was in the same city where the case originated for the landmark 1954 Supreme Court decision wherein the justices unanimously ruled that racial segregation of children in public schools was unconstitutional.)

Not with surprise, I discovered while writing this book that the *Washington for Jesus* rally that I attended in 1988 was purposely held on April 29th in honor of Rev. Robert Hunt's planting of the cross and his prayer of dedication. My Holy Spirit-prompted visit to Virginia Beach in 2007 was only a few months after the 400th year anniversary celebration of the First Landing. The Christian Broadcasting Network (CBN) had a major event that year, and Regent Pictures helped produce the award-winning movie, First Landing. CBN and Regent University are a part of the answer to Rev. Hunt's prayer.

Nehemiah's Blueprint

Just about two months after my encounter with the Lord surrounding this event in history, there was the first-ever discovery of some of the remains of Nehemiah's wall in Israel. What happens in Israel is always an important sign. Nehemiah was appointed as governor over Jerusalem with the permission of the Persian King. Nehemiah had become burdened about the condition of his nation's capital city and the people remaining in it. Even though worship had been restored at the Temple, the walls and gates of the city were still broken down and burnt, and the people were suffering. Previously, Jerusalem had been destroyed by the Babylonians and most of the inhabitants were taken captive in what is modern day Iraq. However, the Persians had then conquered the Babylonian empire.

As mentioned in an earlier chapter, my Releasing Heaven Ministries family has a call to build relationships with the Kurds that live in Northern Iraq (modern-day Assyria). The Lord prompted me before our mission trip there in 2017 to think on Nehemiah and his tie to Esther. An article I found suggested that the Queen mentioned in Nehemiah may have been Esther, and that she may have influenced the king (her stepson) to grant Nehemiah's request to return to Jerusalem with supplies. At the time of the discovery of Nehemiah's wall in 2007, the story of Esther had been the basis of the style of prayer used in the church I was a part of. Most times we would first worship the Lord extensively before any petitions were made. Then with the discovery of Nehemiah's wall, there was a release of at least two additional prophetic revelations: first, the effectiveness of the church is proportionate to the condition of the city in which it resides; and second, in order to build a wall of prayer around our city, each one should first build the wall in front of their own home. In other words, pray for your immediate neighbors and community. At the time of writing this book, the mandate from the Lord to care for our neighbors has become even clearer.

Nehemiah's strategic plan and his refusal to listen to naysayers enabled the wall around Jerusalem to be built in just 52 days. In Nehemiah 8, we see that the restoration of the wall and gates of Jerusalem prepared the entire land and the people to hear and understand the Word of God and to do what was written in it. We can glean then that the restoration of the wall of prayer around the city, and kingdom rule at the gates, the places of authority, the places for justice, business and media, will greatly impact understanding the Word and the Lord's essence—His presence and His heart. The timeline of completion was on the same day of creation, and the time of reading the Law. This was just before the Feast of Tabernacles. Anne Gimenez, who co-led the *Washington for Jesus* rallies with her husband John (who is now home with the Lord), released a word in 2018 that the church has entered into the season of the Feast of Tabernacles. She declared that we have experienced Passover through Salvation in Jesus; and we have experienced Pentecost through the Latter Rain and Charismatic Movements, but now is the time for the Feast of the Ingathering, the Feast of Tabernacles (the feast designated for fruit, joy and harvest). She declared it was time now to move into the fields of harvest.

"I Called You as a Watchman!"

In 2008, I heard the Lord firmly speak, "I called you as a Watchman." I could clearly sense the Lord was telling me that some of the assignments that I had taken on, although good, were not His plan for me. I remember even finding a watch right outside the doorway of my job that evening as I headed to our Watch service. It took about two years before I untangled myself from extra responsibilities; by that time, His grace had completely lifted. I came to understand that all of the things that I had been able to accomplish up to that point were based on His grace and anointing. Obedience indeed is better than sacrifice—an important lesson for us all. I felt not only the Lord's pruning but his re-positioning. I knew instinctively that the blueprints He had laid out from Nehemiah's story were on the horizon.

The Watch fires are being lit

The final revelation for sprouting came through a dream in 2010. I saw watch fires being lit across the northern border of the United States, starting in the Oregon and Washington state areas and then down the East Coast. I also saw the Carolinas and Tennessee on fire for the Lord, as well as other centers in Texas, New Mexico, and Atlanta, Georgia. I followed through on that dream and visited Oregon and Washington State in September 2010. I first spent time in Portland praying specifically for the three key things I had found in my research of the area.

One key thing was the ministry of John G. Lake and the Healing Rooms. John's ministry began in 1898, when his wife was miraculously healed, and continued until his death in 1935. In 1908, he obeyed the Lord's call to South Africa where he ministered until his wife's tragic death in 1913. There are a million converts, over 600 churches, and 1200 ministers attributed to his work in South Africa during those five years. When John returned to the United States in 1914, he settled in Spokane, Washington and shortly thereafter opened a healing room. It is said that 100,000 people were healed there. He later opened a healing room in Portland. The rooms closed at his death in 1935, but in 1999, the Lord called someone to re-open the well of his healing ministry. So one assignment was to pray for the continued success of that ministry.

The second key thing was a possible breach in covenant that occurred with the Azusa Revival. Two of the women connected with Papa Seymour's Apostolic Faith paper moved to Portland in 1909, with the mailing list of his 50,000 subscribers. They also founded a congregation using the same name as Seymour's church in Los Angeles. Initially it seemed as though he gave his blessing; but the end result was that he lost touch with his followers, which caused the eventual decline of the Azusa Street Mission. Consequently, I stood in the gap to repent for the breach and to restore the lines of communication from coast to coast and beyond.

The final key research piece was the pioneer spirit that led people west along the Oregon Trail. I found certain trail markers to pray at. I also drove up and down the highway alongside the Columbia River prophesying a fresh release, fresh fire, and fresh wind of a watchman anointing to sweep across the land, first to the north and then down the East Coast. There was such a pioneer spirit hanging in the atmosphere. I could sense the fullness of the passion, purpose, and persevering endurance of those who initially blazed the trail west.

During this time period, I heard a word from the Lord that I now worked for Him. I also received prophetic words from known prophets about having access to an open heaven and that I was being sent forth as an Ezekiel to bring water to the dry bones. Over the course of the next two years, while I continued to serve at the church I was a part of, I increasingly felt once again "like a stranger in my own city". I knew that I was out of position before the Lord, so finally in October 2012, I laid everything down.

For the Saving of Nations

In Genesis 37, Joseph, a son of Jacob (Israel), had a dream, a promise, a seed of destiny. The dream first led him unwittingly to discord with his brothers, then into a pit of enslavement, and then, through false accusations, to a prison. But through a prophetic act, a dream interpretation, it led him to a palace and to being second in command in all of Egypt.

My prayer is that as you have been reading this "scroll," you have already begun to recognize the seeds of your destiny: the dreams, the visions, the impressions, the living Word, the prophetic signs, the prophetic words, the still small voice, and the knowing that have been on your path, even your present location and the time and place of your birth. I also pray that you have comprehended the importance of covenant, as well as the power and surety of the faithfulness of our very big and very good Heavenly Father.

What transpires next is a specific demonstration of prophecy that universally points to the season, the era we have crossed into. This prophecy relates to the destiny primarily of this nation as it relates to all other nations. As with Joseph, your dream relates to the nation where you find yourself, as well as to the nation where you came from. The Lord is unleashing the storehouses of prayers that have been prayed throughout the ages for a saving of the nations. There is a declarative message from the scroll contained in the journey unfolding next that is beyond my personal story. It bears witness that another Great Awakening is upon us. That Awakening requires a response. As one of the Lord's Watchmen, I echo His call to you, that it is time for your dry bones to arise. At His instruction, I call to the wind of God, the breath of God, to restore your hope, your vision, your hearing, and your understanding. And I decree LIFE!

PART FOUR:

A Planting of the LORD

CHAPTER 15

Suddenly!

AFTER I RECEIVED THAT FIRM REMINDER FROM THE Lord in 2008 about my calling as a Watchman, my eyes were increasingly opened and attentive to His movement, His desires. I remember having various visions during our corporate worship and prayer services. Once, I saw the Lord riding a horse with His hand extended and asking if I would ride with Him. Another time, I could see Him beckoning me to "dance with Me" as I could hear Paul Wilbur's song rolling through my spirit. In addition to my full-time job and organizing or supporting other church events, I had been working in the evenings and weekends for about three years in the bible college with just a handful of full-time students. Although, our classes and special lectures were fairly well-attended, I wondered how effective we had actually been in equipping people to serve the Lord.

I started reflecting on the five-fold gifts listed in Ephesians 4 and wondered, how we could ensure that those gifts are being engaged in our training. I would meet leaders and members of other churches and small groups who had started corporately worshiping and praying. They often testified that since they started a corporate watch, the folks they had been pursuing in outreach were now running to the altar. I was asked to start some outreaches during this season, and we were seeing some results when we followed-up with door-to-door prayer. However, it seemed we were missing the mark. I finally figured out that I was out of position from what the Lord had planned for my next steps. Consequently, late in the evening on October 19, 2012, I made a decision to lay down everything I was doing and wait on Him.

First Dream—A Dream of Two Choices

On the third night after that decision, I had a very vivid and intense dream.

In this dream, I was back in Philadelphia at the major thoroughfare of Broad and Market Streets on the west side of City Hall. I remember being in the plaza and thinking, "broad is the way that leads to destruction." As I headed up Market Street walking towards 19th Street, I was literally in conversation with two of me. I had worked near 19th and Market Streets when I first got out of college, so I knew there was a familiar trolley stop there that could take me towards my family home.

My two selves each had a different opinion: one was to stay above ground, walk to the business district, and forget about home; and the other was to take the stairway down to a dark and lonely platform and wait for my trolley. Going home seemed like the right thing to do, even though the path at first seemed dark. I knew that from this stop, the trolley only rode underground for a short distance; but at a certain place, it would make a hard turn and then climb upward to come out into the light at 40th Street.

I went down to wait, even though I knew a few trolleys would pass me by because they would be full. In reality, it would have made more sense to have boarded the trolley near Broad Street, but it was as if I had to walk those six blocks further. Once on the platform, the Lord prompted me to get on a different trolley. This one did not lead to my home, but instead at 40th street, it made a right turn out of the tunnel. I could see that I was taking it back to the park across from my former pastor's house — the park where my heart cried out for true revival.

When I woke up, I knew it was time to walk out the night vision the Lord gave me in 1990 on my first night in the little town of Bethlehem, Pennsylvania. I knew that the journey would be hard. I wrestled with the thought of feeling inadequate for the task, but I could feel the hand of the Lord upon me. I remember saying (out loud, as I recall), "Yes Lord, we need to release heaven on earth." So that is the how and why Releasing Heaven Ministries (RHM) was birthed. I was so undone after this dream that I stayed home from work the next day.

When I fully said "Yes LORD," one of the additional instructions I received was to "Align with Chuck Pierce." I did not know what that meant and was actually kind of afraid of what that could mean. I did not want to have to go through yet another 15 years of preparation. Nevertheless, I began searching on Glory of Zion's website. First, I found one of their Watch services, and I was amazed that there were other watchmen out there. I then found, after some deep searching, that "align" was a real term that they used. I also discovered that there are actually various ways for people to "align" under Chuck's apostolic covering. Wow!

Second Dream—A Dream of Awakening

The next night, the night I had stayed home from work, I had another very vivid and intense dream.

In this dream, I woke up back in the house I owned in Chester, Pennsylvania. I was disheveled from sleeping, but I knew where I was and that I did not really live there anymore. I left the back area of the house and started walking towards the front of the house. There wasn't any furniture in the house, but I could see what I used to have there in my mind's eye. That house had a lot of windows along the full length of one side. It was a VERY bright, sunny day. Floods of living light just poured into the house. There was hope, peace, joy, delight, assurance, and worship in that light. I began passing through the dining room as I was heading towards the front of house. Once under the archway between the dining room and living room, there was a downpour of water from above. Before I could ask, two men were there to help. One asked if he could help me; and the other without asking just went to the basement and fell down the steps. He was in a suit. He apparently fell flat and came back to the dining room covered in dust. Somehow, the front door was slightly ajar and four dogs of various sizes, colorings, breeds entered. The big, black dog jumped on me and urinated – wow. I then felt an urgency to get upstairs to find the source of water.

In those moments, I remembered that the archway was where I had a visitation from the Lord. A few weeks prior to that visitation, I had a word from a prophet that the Lord wanted to visit me but He didn't want to scare me. The visitation occurred around 1993 before I moved to Tulsa. Because a family member was staying with me then, I was actually sleeping in the living room. I was asleep but I could somehow still see. I saw the dining room fill up with about 8-10 angels. They were hard to count because they were too big for the room and they were cloaked. I watched as this escalator suddenly appeared, and a man started coming down this escalator. As He began to approach where the ceiling had been, the angels bowed and proclaimed, "He's here." I somehow then saw the Lord walk over to where I was sleeping and He just watched me rest. I could feel this wellspring of great love, pleasure, and joy. He was like a dad checking in on his little girl and watching her as she rested and perhaps dreamed.

In the dream, as I went upstairs to find the source of water, I was really sensing that this was an outpouring from heaven, and that I would not actually find a faucet left on or a pipe that burst. In the natural when I lived in this house, it had been converted to a duplex. While in the dream there was now easy access to the upstairs; in actuality, I would have had to go outside to go to a separate entryway and exterior door. As I moved towards this stairwell from the inside, I remembered that I had a tenant. Once in the stairwell, it was as if I entered another dimension. The stairs themselves were made of beautiful rich wood and there was beautiful wood paneling with magnificent ornate carvings on them. When I reached the top of the stairs, the room I saw was this huge; it was an unending open kitchen with boiling pots steaming on the stove, beautifully ornate wooden cabinetry, and many, many, many tables of various styles and sizes. Some of the tables would seat two, some four, some six, and some looked like they would seat eight or more. I commented to my "tenant" how I loved what she had done with the place. I somehow "remembered" that her name was "Syreeta." (I never actually had a tenant of that name. I looked the name up later and found out it meant "companion" and "to flow like a river.")

Syreeta was busy cooking and did not seem to mind that I was disheveled, drenched with the water that was pouring out downstairs, and peed on. I had a puzzled look on my face as I was looking at the many tables, the pots on the stove, and the breath-taking décor while quietly wondering what she was doing. She answered my unspoken question and said that she was preparing this meal for my family and that I needed to go back and invite them. I somehow knew that my family included some natural members, but mainly spiritual ones—those I knew plus those I had not yet met, including some who did not know the Lord yet.

I went back downstairs planning to help the guy who had fallen down the steps. His suit was just covered in dirt and dust. I felt that I should at least get his suit cleaned, but I was prompted instead to focus on the task of letting my family know that they had been invited to dine with the Lord.

As I was adding this second dream to this scroll, I paused to seek the Lord about including the parts about the dogs and the guy falling down the steps. Through an interpretation from the Lord, I later recognized the dogs as specific people, and the two men who stepped in to help as different structures. The first man was a servant, Spirit-led, and humble; and the other, although well-meaning, moved out of just knowledge and tradition, a type of a religious spirit. As your heart gets stirred and you are awakened by Him, you will face opposition in various forms. The Lord wants you to know that this awakening is still Him. Stepping into the deeper things of God stirs opposition. Satan and his demonic forces do not want you really to understand that you have great authority over the kingdom of this world. All the heroes of the faith faced opposition. Abraham did, Joseph did, Moses did, Joshua and Caleb did, Esther did, Nehemiah did, and even Jesus, our King of Glory, did. It comes down to whose report will you believe. What you are feeling and what you are sensing have been written in the Scriptures beforehand. It has been written in the annals of time. If the Lord broke through once, He will do it again. Just ask Him to confirm. He is always there, He is faithful, and He is good.

Here is a Scripture reference for what I encountered: Ephesians 5: 13-17 (CJB), "But everything exposed to the light is revealed clearly for what it is, since anything revealed is a light. This is why it says, 'Get up, sleeper! Arise from the dead, and the Messiah will shine on you!' Therefore, pay careful attention to how you conduct your life — live wisely, not unwisely. Use your time well, for these are evil days. So don't be foolish, but try to understand what the will of the Lord is."

A Second Time

At the end of 2018, the Lord had me look at Glory of Zion's Day 17 Gaining Access Watch. As they started worshiping, I was reminded of this second dream. Then confirming words began to come forth about how the Lord was inviting us to the banqueting table so we can come and dine with Him. Below is the Lord's message from reviewing this second dream a second time:

Wake up!! Light is flooding in. Heaven is pouring out. He will send you help, but discern the help. He is truly preparing a banqueting table for you, even in the presence of your enemies. It is important to note that an enemy is anyone who tries to stop your mission. Jesus had to rebuke Peter when Peter spoke against Jesus' going to the cross. There is a stairway for you leading up to where He is seated. That stairway is the masterpiece of your destiny. Holy Spirit is preparing the meal in the realm that the world cannot see, BUT you really can see it. Holy Spirit is the Helper. Holy Spirit is asking us on behalf of the king, our Jesus, to invite our family. It is a supernatural, loving act with gifts like this dream. For me, I am a seer prophet who sees visions and dreams, but we all can hear from the Lord, receive dreams and impressions, get quickened by Scripture, or receive a word of knowledge or wisdom. The Lord looks at people as "family," and we are on a search and rescue mission. It will be their choice as to whether they accept His invitation. He is leaving the religious spirit behind – there is a separation going on. I had a vision during one of our Watches during the same month of my dreams but two years later. In this vision, I saw the Lord establishing His kingdom, house to house. There were members of what appeared to be a large local denominational church who were falling weeping at the altar and casting aside their religious garbs and protocol. I then saw them returning to their homes wrapped in the dew of humility, taking up the Word of God, and worshiping Him there.

What Time was this "Suddenly" on God's Calendar?

As I finished writing this chapter, I was led to look up the month and year on God's calendar that this "Suddenly!" occurred in. As you will see below and as I mentioned in an earlier chapter, I did follow the Lord's instructions to align with Chuck Pierce through Glory of Zion International. The Lord has given Chuck and the ministry there revelation on how to align with

His calendar. As I noted previously, Emperor Constantine had gotten the church off of God's calendar which is detailed in Scripture—both the calendar and the action of trying to change the calendar are written in Scripture. Two Scriptures come to mind: Genesis 1: 14 (NIV), And God said, "Let there be lights in the vault of the sky to separate the day from the night, and let them serve as signs to mark sacred times, and days and years," and Daniel 7: 24b-25(NIV), After them another king will arise, different from the earlier ones; he will subdue three kings. [25] He will speak against the Most High and oppress his holy people and try to change the set times and the laws. The holy people will be delivered into his hands for a time, times and half a time. Glory of Zion, as well as other ministries, are helping the Body of Christ move back into rhythm with the Lord. I liken this teaching to putting your cup fully under the water faucet to get all that the Lord is pouring out. Chuck's book A Time to Advance written with Robert and Linda Heidler as well as Robert's book The Messianic Church Arising! give really excellent foundational and prophetic teaching on God's calendar.

The month and year of my dreams was October 22-23, 2012, which was in the month of Cheshvan in the Hebraic year 5773. Here is the prophetic meaning of the year from Glory of Zion's advertisement for their Head of the Year Conference for 5773: "The Camels are Coming—A Year to Bridge the Past and the Future and Move from Recovery to Wholeness! This will be the year of Ayin Gimel (73). Gimel is the third letter of the Hebrew alphabet as well as the number 3, and originally pictured a camel. This is a year that we will be looking for the camels to come! This is a time to keep your feet moving and go beyond where you have been in the past, until you drink and eat of the produce of your promise! The Kingdom of God will become the greatest influence in the earth realm." From one of Robert's teachings about the decade of Ayin (70), Ayin is the picture of an eye. We are to look again, see again, and see what we could not see before. We are to see into the realms that we had not seen before. 'Angels', also known as watchers, is an <u>ayin</u> word. And the number 70 represents empowerment and release; the Lord will show Himself strong. Moreover, <u>Cheshvan</u> is the month of Noah's flood—the month it started in one year and also the month the waters subsided in the next. One of the aligned ones of Glory of Zion had this revelation about the month of <u>Cheshvan</u>, "… Because Noah followed what God said, which by the way went beyond his understanding, there was an ark prepared so that God could shut the door on their past and launch them into the future."

Amen. An accurate picture of where I found myself—at the end and at the beginning. I was given a word that Friday night prior to my decision to leave my former church, and indeed, it came to pass. "Come, and let us return to the Lord; For He has torn, but He will heal us; He has stricken, but He will bind us up. After two days He will revive us; On the third day He will raise us up, That we may live in His sight." (Hosea 6:1-2, NKJV)

CHAPTER 16

Tapping into the Fullness of Christ

Alignment—"Align with Chuck Pierce"

AS I MENTIONED EARLIER, WHEN I FULLY SAID "YES LORD," one of the additional instructions that I received was to "Align with Chuck Pierce." *Align* was not a familiar *Christian* term for me, so I started digging on Glory of Zion's website. After clicking on various links, I came across their Tuesday morning prayer service webcast. The time of day piqued my interest. I was catching the replay at 6:00 am, and that service had already occurred at 3:00 am. (There really is something quite special about those wee hours of the morning. I have received angelic visitations and some of the clearest revelation during those hours. It is like the city is really asleep and I can almost hear heaven's whispers.) The prayer service that I watched was full of a harp and bowl style worship and prophetic declarations fashioned after the style of worship going on in heaven (Revelation 5:8-14). In the worship in heaven, the music never stops and in the midst of that sound, there are songs, declarations of admiration, and decrees of what has been, what is and what is to come.

And in the service I watched, they called themselves watchmen. I had found my tribe! The Lord trained me to watch and pray, so my inner man was reverberating with their joyful, gloriously triumphant sound. I heard the mindset of being His legislative assembly as well as His army. I heard wisdom, authority, and identity—son, priest, and king. I heard fire and boldness. I heard apostolic decrees and passion for His kingdom and His righteousness. I saw spiritual gifts in operation, including speaking declarative messages in tongues with the interpretation following. I had not witnessed that level of a flow with the gift of tongues in decades. I saw women leaders, the generations, the nations, and prophetic movement (dance, flags and more)! I saw a company that engaged heaven. They were indeed amongst those called to co-labor with the Lord to repair the breaches and to rebuild the waste places.

I was really alert then, so I also took the time to watch the replay of their Sunday morning service. That service was about Gideon and how to walk in strength. It was about knowing who you are, getting direction from God, and dealing with sin the Lord's way. The teacher that morning proclaimed, "The Lord is not looking for perfection but a pure heart." The instruction was simply to take a step of faith and to seek His strategy—amen! I now even more eagerly kept searching until I found the Zion Connect section that described *five* ways that people could *align*: individually, as a small group, a ministry, a church, and even a business. I immediately requested more information about what was required to align. In the reply I received just a couple of days later, I found statements that they are a network for those called to be in the apostolic-prophetic sphere. The Zion Connect Questionnaire Form asked about giftings and relationships with others in your own region or territory. The questionnaire for a ministry asked about vision and mission. There was mention of equipping resources and prayer focuses. This was a refreshing approach. It was centered on the Lord's calling versus certificates, diplomas, and degrees.

One of the many blessings that alignment has brought is the global gatherings. Dutch Sheets, a frequent speaker, has taught us that the word *alignment* is <u>katartizo</u> in Greek. He stated, "It means to put something into its proper position. It is the word for mending a broken bone, setting a dislocated one back in place. It has to do with equipping the saints as described in Ephesians 4. When you come into proper alignment, you are equipped to do what God has called you to do. But what most of you do not know is that the word also means 'to finish.'"

About a year after my "Yes Lord," I was asked what I would say the key advantage of aligning with Chuck had been. In addition to recapturing the missing pieces of revival history, getting back in the rhythm of God's calendar (including His appointed times), and honoring even more fully God's First Nation Israel—all of which have had a HUGE impact on my life—I would still say that having the Ephesians 4 Christ-giftings or Christ-anointings operational, as it is written in Scripture, is a game-changer. Having the new wineskin, especially with true apostles as a critical part of the foundation, fully functional and available has been something missing in my previous church experiences. I remember even noticing on a recent visit to the Billy Graham Library that there was an ellipsis replacing the words "apostles, prophets" on a wall placard that displayed the Ephesians 4:11 Scripture. Billy Graham is one of my heroes of the faith, a spiritual father to our nation. He was such a powerful and humble servant who honored Holy Spirit, knew the power of prayer and discipleship, understood the power of having a team, and honored Jesus and the Written Word of God above all else. The way he organized crusades and tapped into the media of the day was simply outstanding. I recently watched a documentary that included testimonies of how Billy Graham did not allow his crusades to be segregated, even though it was technically illegal for him to do so. It also spoke about how he traveled to even nations that were our perceived enemies for the sake of preaching the gospel. I have watched his crusades only on television; but I was told by an eyewitness that the one held in Charlotte in the Panthers' stadium in 1996, which drew 330,000 attendees plus 25,000 volunteers from 900 churches representing over 54 denominations across both North and South Carolina, was simply electrifying. Yet, my home city of Philadelphia, and also Charlotte, have not been what I would call transformed. I believe stepping into the restoration of apostles and prophets will extend the powerful forerunning work of the great evangelists, pastors, and teachers like Billy Graham, William Branham, Jack Coe, and others, and even multiply the impact.

Scripture tells us that apostles and prophets are a part of our foundation along with Jesus. Ephesians 2:19-22 (NIV): "Consequently, you are no longer foreigners and strangers, but fellow citizens with God's people and also members of his household, built on the foundation of the apostles and prophets, with Christ Jesus himself as the chief cornerstone. In him the whole building is joined together and rises to become a holy temple in the Lord. And in him you too are being built together to become a dwelling in which God lives by his Spirit." God's five-fold government rule requires reliance on Holy Spirit and the function of His gifts. Its focus is on bringing forth the Kingdom. Matthew 6:33 tells us to seek first His kingdom and His righteousness. Matthew 6:10 teaches us to pray to the Father for His kingdom to come, His will to be done on the earth as it is in heaven. Even Daniel 7:13-14, 18 (NIV) describes what this looks like: "As my vision continued that night, I saw someone like a son of man coming with the clouds of heaven. He approached the Ancient One and was led into his presence. He was given authority, honor, and sovereignty over all the nations of the world, so that people of every race and nation and language would obey him. His rule is eternal—it will never end. His Kingdom will never be destroyed. But in the end, the holy people of the Most High will be given the Kingdom, and they will rule forever and ever."

Secured in the Root of Covenant

We Gentiles are grafted into God's Covenant with Abraham by the blood of Jesus (Ephesians 2:11-13, Ephesians 2:19, Ephesians 3:6, Romans 11:17-24). Derek Prince has excellent teachings and a list of declarations about what the Blood of the Lamb has secured for us. But there is a fullness promised via alignment and equipping (Ephesians 4:11-16).

From Glory of Zion's new website, "The promise of the one new man goes beyond gender, race, and ethnicity. In fact, its foundation is found when we let go of our worldly representations and bring down the walls that would keep our gifts separated and our spirits bound to a legalistic, worldly structure. This has been proven to us through the work of the cross. Christ's ultimate sacrifice grafted us into a promise and inheritance to forever reconcile our hearts in eternity with our everlasting Father. And with that hope in our hearts, we step boldly into an unknown future – one that will move us closer to our Father's heart with every step of faith we take – until we reach the manifested promise and fullness of our lives in Christ Jesus our Savior."

I personally aligned with Glory of Zion right away. Within about three months, I was aligned as both a House of Zion, which covered our house fellowship meetings where we webcast Glory of Zion's services, and as a Ministry of Zion, which covered our team's full vision and mission of shifting the atmosphere over our region and other assigned locations using the Lord's strategy of worship, prayer and outreach. When the Lord brought Releasing Heaven Ministries (RHM) forth, He called me as an apostle. However, as C. Peter Wagner explained, although spiritual authority resides with the apostle, that apostle must be aligned with another apostle and be accountable to him or her. The basis for the definition that I have used in our documents can be found in Chuck Pierce and Robert Heidler's book <u>The Apostolic Church Arising</u>. An apostle is the God-appointed spiritual leader within the five-fold ministry gifts (apostles, prophets, teachers, pastors, and evangelists) and operates supernaturally in close relationship with Jesus and Holy Spirit to interpret what God is doing in a territory (to intercede for it, steward it) and to set the church in order. An apostolic church is vision-oriented. Those in fellowship have their needs met, but the goal is for every believer to be trained, to be equipped, and to move forward toward his or her God-ordained destiny.

Earlier I noted that Anne Gimenez, who co-led the Washington for Jesus rallies, released a word in 2018 that the church had entered into the season of the Feast of Tabernacles. She declared that we have experienced Passover through Salvation in Jesus, and we have experienced Pentecost through the Latter Rain and Charismatic Movements; but now was the time for the Feast of the Ingathering, the Feast of Tabernacles, the feast designated for fruit, joy, and harvest. She declared it was time now to move into the fields of harvest. So our portion for the Body of Christ is as the company of tribes of Judah, Issachar, and Zebulun, who were camped to the east of the Tabernacle in the Wilderness. Those tribes carried an anointing for worship, for prophetic decrees based in seeing and understanding, and for breakthrough access to the needed resources for advancement.

We have found that our assignment and alignment are doing just that for the Body of Christ in our region, our nation, and the nations where we have been sent. The Scriptures tell us to not despise small beginnings, to be faithful in little, and to be patient as our gifts will make room for us and bring us before even kings. For our House of Zion, we started out with gatherings of two or more folks in my home twice a month. Then separately, we gathered corporately in Charlotte on the third Saturday of each month for worship and Watch-type prayer. We also would meet on the fourth weekend at various sites (an Indian Reservation, a former local plantation, the square at Trade & Tryon Streets, the Charlotte Mecklenburg Government Center, the Charleston

Market, Raleigh, Columbia, colleges, and universities) for prayers of repentance and restoration. In addition, we encouraged and trained others to do similar Watch-type prayers in their homes and communities at least once a month, and we connected with and assisted others who have similar missions, visions, and statements of faith.

After about two and a half years, at the direction of the Lord, Releasing Heaven Ministries (RHM) transitioned its Worship and Prayer Gatherings. We moved out county to county throughout the Carolinas to release whirlwinds of His glory and to truly connect earth with heaven's rule and reign in our region. Then about a year after that, in fulfillment of our call as a Local and Regional Apostolic Center, Releasing Heaven Ministries launched Ephesians 4 Movement (E4M), which includes equipping activities and outreaches. We have traveled from Charleston, Beaufort, Greenville, and Edgefield counties in South Carolina to Dare, Onslow, Henderson, Burke, Cherokee, Jackson, and the Charlotte Metro area counties in North Carolina. We also journeyed to Philadelphia, Pennsylvania; Kingsport and Nashville, Tennessee; New Echota, Georgia; Paris and Logan County, Kentucky; and to Haiti, Italy, France, Germany, Israel, and Modern Day Assyria. We have hosted outreaches locally—releasing worship and prayer in the center of Uptown Charlotte, in a field in a housing project via a block party in a drug-ridden community, in a convenience store parking lot that has been the site of gang-related killings, in a church parking lot in a neighborhood that had transitioned from affluence to poverty over the years, at University of North Carolina at Charlotte and Queens University of Charlotte. We have prayer-walked our colleges and universities from Wilmington to Greensboro to Columbia to Charleston and those locally. We have released the blessings of past revivals from Billy Graham to Alfred Garr to the Waldensians (who founded Valdese, NC) to the Moravians (who founded Bethlehem, PA and Old Salem, NC) to Jacksonville and Eastern North Carolina (agreeing with Derek

Prince's prophecy about the revival that would be birthed there) to Virginia Beach (agreeing with Rev. Robert Hunt's prayers for our land). In other words, we have taken these things seriously.

If you are not familiar with prayer-walks, you might find it strange that we would take prayer journeys to other places. You may wonder if there is any impact, anything different about the location of the prayers. When I lived in Philadelphia, the church I attended regularly prayer-walked our community. In the spirit, I could readily see a lasso of light encircling the streets where we walked. In Scripture, you can see a pattern about land and boundaries. Even God's promise to Abraham included a very specific place for him to dwell. The Lord cut covenant with Abraham as a guarantee about the land. Genesis 15: 7-8 (NIV), He also said to him, "I am the Lord, who brought you out of Ur of the Chaldeans to give you this land to take possession of it." But Abram said, "Sovereign Lord, how can I know that I will gain possession of it?" So the Lord said to him, "Bring me a heifer, a goat and a ram, each three years old, along with a dove and a young pigeon." You also see in Scripture where Abraham memorialized certain places of encounters with the Lord. There may have been a well dug or an altar built. These were places of Worship. How we deal with our worship and our relationships impacts the land, which can be seen even from the fall in the garden. Genesis 3:15 (AMP): "And I will put enmity between you and the woman, and between your offspring and her Offspring; He will bruise and tread your head underfoot, and you will lie in wait and bruise His heel." Chuck released a prophetic word sometime around the start of Releasing Heaven Ministries, which was confirmation for me. He stated, "And I say My harvest fields are two layers down. Therefore you must remove the iniquity out of the ground, and as the iniquity flees, the seed you've sown will begin to rise. I say to you open your eyes for I will use you like I used Judah to plow the fields that were sown in other generations."

We have authority in our feet to both root out the enemy and to build a homestead. Deuteronomy 11:22-24 (NIV): If you carefully observe all these commands I am giving you to follow—to love the Lord your God, to walk in obedience to him and to hold fast to him— then the Lord will drive out all these nations before you, and you will dispossess nations larger and stronger than you. Every place where you set your foot will be yours: Your territory will extend from the desert to Lebanon, and from the Euphrates River to the Mediterranean Sea.

Then other Scriptures tell us what is actually happening behind the scenes when we pray. We see that there are territorial boundaries. Daniel 10:12-14 (NIV): Then he continued, "Do not be afraid, Daniel. Since the first day that you set your mind to gain understanding and to humble yourself before your God, your words were heard, and I have come in response to them. But the prince of the Persian kingdom resisted me twenty-one days. Then Michael, one of the chief princes, came to help me, because I was detained there with the king of Persia. Now I have come to explain to you what will happen to your people in the future, for the vision concerns a time yet to come."

As a result of pressing in and completing our assignments (worshiping out of our whole hearts and submitting ourselves to wholly follow the Lord's will and instructions regardless of the time or financial commitment required), we have helped to open some special portals from past generations. We have encountered angelic activity and the Presence of the Lord in such a powerful measure that it has shouted to us so loudly that Awakening is at hand.

What I mean by portals is that we can see in Scripture that there are certain places on earth that have been so consecrated that heavenly visitation can more readily come. In Genesis 28:10-15 (ESV), Jacob left Beersheba and went toward Haran. And he came to a **certain place** and stayed there that night, because the sun had set. **Taking one of the stones of the place**, he put it under his head and lay down in that place to sleep. And he dreamed, and behold, there was a ladder set up on the earth, and the top of it reached to heaven. And behold, the angels of God were ascending and descending on it! And behold, the LORD stood above it and said, "I am the LORD, the God of Abraham your father and the God of Isaac. The land on which you lie I will give to you and to your offspring. Your offspring shall be like the dust of the earth, and you shall spread abroad to the west and to the east and to the north and to the south, and in you and your offspring shall all the families of the earth be blessed. Behold, I am with you and will keep you wherever you go, and will bring you back to this land. For I will not leave you until I have done what I have promised you." That certain place was in the region that the Lord had made a covenantal promise to Abraham, so Abraham had built an altar to the Lord there (Genesis 12:7-8). Abraham returned a second time to extend more worship to the Lord (Genesis 13:3–4). The Scripture does not indicate that Jacob intentionally stopped there, but it was a consecrated place that the Lord and all of heaven honored. The angels ascended and descended there, and in the midst of that, the Lord repeated His covenant promise to Jacob that He made to Abraham.

The Lord gave Dutch Sheets the term "synergy of the ages." In one of the global conferences held at Glory of Zion, Dutch shared that the connecting of the ages can be seen in the Scriptures about those in the Hebrews' hall of faith. Hebrews 11:39-40 (NIV): "These were all commended for their faith, yet none of them received what had been promised, since God had planned something better for us so that only together with us would they be made perfect." The Lord caused Dutch to understand that if we agree with the generations past, it will multiply power. Dutch surmised that to mean that we will not get only what they had, but we'll get what they had multiplied. He shared that Julie Meyer, who at the time was one of the worship leaders at the International House of Prayer, also received a similar concept in a dream about angels, ambulances, and intercessors. In Julie's dream, when the angels told those weary, fainting intercessors the old, old stories of the past revivals, their heart beat and their strength were restored. The message of her dream was that we need to embrace the old, old stories as our story. Dutch remarked that, "Covenant is what enables us to connect. This is not about wanting my generation to have revival, this is about covenantal faithfulness from generation to generation."

At another time, Dutch shared a dream that someone else had who shared the dream with him because he was in it. It was about the generations and covenant. In that dream, the Lord also used the phrase "synergy of the ages." That person did not know that God had also given that same term to Dutch. There were six generations in this dream, including Dutch, Billy Graham, and others representing one of the present generations. There were also people who were the pilgrims, the pioneers, and the planters. The message from that dream was that "America is returning to the ancient path to reap the harvest of the ages." Dutch pondered what could God have promised our forefathers knowing that it would not be fulfilled in their generation. Dutch further commented, "This is why I think prophecy is so important—the prophetic taps into God's eternal nature and gets outside time and sees the future and comes back into time and tells us what it is." I recommend you get ahold of Dutch's An Appeal to Heaven book to read the whole dream.

For me, that dream helped me understand the visions some have had about a tsunami wave hitting America. In my mind's eye, I could see myself alone on a beach facing a great storm with great thunderings, very dark clouds, and a huge billowing wave rolling towards me. My strength seemed way too small to stop that great storm. My prayers were swallowed up in the sound and appearance of that massive storm. The shore and the land were overtaken. But then, I saw myself making a comeback. I was approaching the shore riding an ever-increasing wave of beautiful water that gained strength because it contained not just my prayers but also the prayers of generation after generation after generation, including Jesus' prayers, Nehemiah's prayers, Esther's prayers, Joshua's prayers, Moses' prayers, Joseph's prayers, and Abraham's prayers. The wave I was riding grew higher, more massive, and more powerful. I knew that I now had the strength to take back the land. I was not alone. There was a covenantal promise, the synergy of the ages, and the ancient ways of prophecy, prayer, worship, Holy Spirit, angel armies, faith, courage, and obedience.

CHAPTER 17

A Trunk of Prayers and Sacrificial Obedience—Their Fire Still Burns

"Watchman, whenever you hear a word from me give them warning" (Ezekiel 33:7, paraphrased)

Revelation 5:6-10 (NIV): Then I saw a Lamb, looking as if it had been slain, standing at the center of the throne, encircled by the four living creatures and the elders. The Lamb had seven horns and seven eyes, which are the seven spirits of God sent out into all the earth. He went and took the scroll from the right hand of him who sat on the throne. And when he had taken it, the four living creatures and the twenty-four elders fell down before the Lamb. Each one had a harp and they were holding golden bowls full of incense, which are the prayers of God's people. And they sang a new song, saying: "You are worthy to take the scroll and to open its seals, because you were slain, and with your blood you purchased for God persons from every tribe and language and people and nation. You have made them to be a kingdom and priests to serve our God, and they will reign on the earth."

Revelation 6:9-10 (NIV): When he opened the fifth seal, I saw under the altar the souls of those who had been slain because of the word of God and the testimony they had maintained. They called out in a loud voice, "How long, Sovereign Lord, holy and true, until you judge the inhabitants of the earth and avenge our blood?" Then each of them was given a white robe, and they were told to wait a little longer, until the full number of their fellow servants, their brothers and sisters, were killed just as they had been.

I know that this is a shocking way to open up some really great news for those of us who believe and have been waiting for our prayers for Awakening to be answered. My Watchman call and the Scriptures in Ezekiel that tell me of my responsibility have weighed on me heavily. A part of the story—our story—that we are tapping into has come at a great price. There are many who seemingly never were able to receive direct blessings from their labors of love. However, we are eternal and connected. Within the stories, the prophetic encounters and prayer assignments below are the truth that the Lord sees outside of time. He sees each of us both individually and corporately. He is building an eternal city that holds His garden that is full of the beauty and glory He placed within the nations He created. It is a truth that shows that we are indeed made in His image. He made us strong and fearless, yet full of the awe and delight that can be seen in a child's eyes. The Lord is faithful, good, kind, patient, and full of love, joy, and peace. He is a righteous and holy God and Father. He is a King who rules with justice and mercy. When I have spoken with other people of various ages, races, and genders, some have not heard these stories. We have neglected the covenantal heritage of Abraham and the ancient way of teaching our children about the mighty deeds and great works of the Lord (Genesis 18:19; Psalm 145:4). As my dad would say, "If you know your history, the sense of who you really are can never be taken away from you."

"Go See About the Constitution"

At the birth of this ministry, the Lord reconnected me with my spiritual sister Susan. It was Susan's family, especially her mother Ann, with whom I spent much time in my early Christian walk. We have always been fanatical about prayer because we knew its power. We knew that the Lord saved us and delivered us through prayer, and we wanted to see His kingdom more fully manifested in the lives of our families, in the neighborhoods of our city, and in our nation. We lost touch through the years, but Momma Ann tracked me down in Charlotte. For the trip the Lord assigned me to take to Glory of Zion's Start the Year Off Right Conference in December 2012, I traveled through Pennsylvania. I arranged my flight so that I could spend a few hours with my spiritual family. I remember that while we were sitting just chatting and laughing, I received the email from North Carolina State approving Releasing Heaven Ministries (RHM) as a non-profit corporation. This was a prophetic sign for me that the Lord was restoring what had seemingly been lost when I had followed the path of His Training Plan. Both Momma Ann and Susan are now a key part of our RHM team. The people the Lord binds us to, the places where we were born, and the places He sends us to live are all significant. And His timing to connect the dots is impeccable!

Somewhere along the way in those first few months, Susan invited me to come to her home in Wilmington, Delaware to train her Friday night ministry group on Watching Prayer. As I had mentioned in previous sections, this type of prayer creates the atmosphere of heaven as seen in Revelation 5 in the earthly realm. Sounds of praise and adoration are intermingled with the proclamations written in Scripture or received by prophecy; and as a result, angelic activity springs forth (Acts 2:3, 5:17-20, 12:5-17, 16:25-30). Jeremiah 29:7 is a part of our foundation to pray in authority, "Also, seek the peace and prosperity of the city to which I have carried you into exile. Pray to the Lord for it, because if it prospers, you too will prosper." Typically, in alignment with Daniel 7:27, 1 Peter 2:9, Revelation 5:10, as priests we center on repenting for actions that stop blessings such as iniquity (willful sin), shedding of innocent blood, or broken covenants; and as kings we seek to understand through research and preparatory prayer what planned destiny we can unlock.

So I traveled there just a few months later. As we were setting things up for the training session, Susan told me about how the Lord had directed her and her husband to buy their home, because it was very strategically placed. She opened the blinds and there before us was Downtown Wilmington. Against the night backdrop with the office lights of all the various buildings, it almost felt like we could reach out and touch the city. Delaware is known as the Business Capital of the United States; more than 50% of all U.S. publicly traded companies and 63% of the Fortune 500 are incorporated there. In my preparatory research, I rediscovered the in-depth history of our Constitution. Delaware was the first state to ratify our Constitution, and they did so unanimously. I could feel the weightiness of that decision, realizing that our Constitution is a covenant. I recognized the blessing of prosperity that fell on Delaware was a type of reward for their obedience. We made plans for me to return with our worship leader, Doris, later that year during Labor Day weekend.

During my preparation time for that second trip, the Lord spoke in my spirit, "Go see about the Constitution." Consequently, I spent several days reading and praying over copies of the Constitution, the Bill of Rights, other Amendments, and the Declaration of Independence, which I printed out along with the names of the Signers and the names of our Presidents. My plan was to lay those things at the altar during our Worship time there. Later, I was pleasantly surprised to find out that there is now a National Constitution Center right on Independence Mall in Philadelphia. Therefore, I made plans to do a Strategic Prayer

AN OAK OF RIGHTEOUSNESS

Outing to discretely pray there, as well as at several of the other historic sites in that immediate area.

During our worship time for that Gathering, I remember feeling impressed by the Lord about how He purposely placed the people who were with us that night in that region to watch over the birthplace of our nation. The Constitution was written and signed in Philadelphia in the Assembly Room of the Pennsylvania State House, now known as Independence Hall. That was the same place the Declaration of Independence was signed.

I expressed to the Gathering attendees what I was sensing as I laid out some of the history of our beginnings as a nation. I told them about my encounter with the story of Rev. Robert Hunt while in Virginia Beach several years back. I told them how Rev. Hunt brought a cross on the ship, required all those on the ship to fast and pray before disembarking, and once on shore, made their first act a prayer meeting to dedicate the land to the Lord. I told them how their prayer included a decree about preaching the gospel to the natives there, as well as sending it forth to the nations of the world. I told them about the Mayflower Compact and the covenant made there. I discussed the many different pastors and congregations who came to America so that they could worship the Lord freely. The early settlers wanted to create "a city on a hill" for Him. I told them about how the nation was birthed out of the First Great Awakening, and how the Lord's hand was on us now to be able to win that war though we were less trained, less equipped, and fewer in numbers. I told them how Acts 17:26-27 declares that we are of one blood, and that the Lord has pre-appointed our times and boundaries so that we would come to know Him. I told them what that meant to me personally—how it no longer mattered to me how I got here because I knew that God had a plan. I told them that even though Washington, D.C. is our current capital, the nation was forged in Philadelphia, and they have a responsibility to watch over not just the city but also the nation.

In the river of the Spirit that was released, we laid hold of the vision that had birthed this nation. We spoke about Julie Meyer's dream with the ambulances, angels and intercessors and the need to tell the old, old stories of revival. Several of them got it and began to pray with authority over the atmosphere of the region as a people representing our covenant with God.

Covenant, Prayer, Gold Coins, and Worship

The morning after the Gathering, we planned a trip to the National Constitution Center. That morning as I was waking up, I saw gold coins being tossed into a hopper, so I declared, "Yes Lord, we will also go to the US Mint."

We first stopped at the Federal Reserve Bank and then went through the National Constitution Center, praying along the entire way. While at the National Constitution Center, we could feel the weighty significance of this Covenant over our nation. There were rooms with statues and other displays showing the lengthy deliberations that took place at that time. I remember Dutch Sheets indicating that Benjamin Franklin, who was the least religious of our Founding Fathers, had called the assembly to daily prayer. He reasoned that if it took prayer to win the war, then how could they think to establish our government without God.

When we walked into the US Mint, we looked up to see a coin display dangling from the ceiling, reminiscent of the scene from my vision. I had forgotten that this was one of the mints that actually still produced our legal tender coins. We went on the self-guided tour and saw some interesting facts about how President Franklin D. Roosevelt issued an Executive Order in 1933 during the depression forcing people to turn in their gold to the Federal Reserve Bank at a much reduced price. It became illegal to own gold until President Ford issued a proclamation in 1974. We noticed that Fort Knox where the gold has been kept since then was not regularly inspected. We pondered those things in our hearts and found later that prophetic words mirroring this encounter had been received by key leaders. We prayed in the Spirit for repentance to come and for justice to prevail.

We then made our way toward Independence Hall and stopped at Christ Church burial grounds. We found some history there about how the freedom to worship had been included in the charter of the city, and how this emerging, small community became home to many churches from a variety of Christian denominations. Philadelphia was even the birthplace (1740) of the oldest, still active Jewish synagogue in the United States. As we entered into the courtyard of Independence Hall, we could sense the Lord's pleasure. We knew there was a connection between this posture of worship and the establishment of our nation's government there. In the Spirit, I could actually see the Lord setting His throne down over our nation, right there in Independence Hall Square.

I then remembered reading a quote by Benjamin Franklin, who was friends with the revivalist George Whitefield, about how one could hear worship pouring out from house to house as one walked down the streets. I found out later through one of Dutch Sheets' messages that William Penn, who founded Pennsylvania, actually asked the Lord for his colony to become the seed of the nation. Dutch remarked that William Penn stands out in history as a man who understood and respected God's covenants. Penn based the government of his colony on covenant. Dutch shared an excerpt from one of William Penn's first legislative acts, and its basis on the Christian faith is quite clear. Dutch further proclaimed, "History matters. Marx even said, 'if I can steal their history, I can steal their nation.'"

"I want you to go to a town in the Northwest corner of Italy near the border of France."

This is what I heard in my spirit in January 2014. I immediately said "yes." I did some research, but I could not seem to find the town. Consequently, I set the assignment in my future pending pile. However, the impressions grew in intensity. I happened to read Peter Wagner's <u>The Queen's Domain: Advancing God's Kingdom in the 40/70 Window</u> book during this time, and I began to understand the significance of what was happening throughout Europe. In June, I even found another prayer journey companion. While at Glory of Zion in Texas on the last day of the Pentecost Celebration Conference, I become re-acquainted with a former elder of my church in Philadelphia, who was now a pastor. Upon mentioning this impression from the Lord, she immediately said, "I believe I am to go with you." But, where was that exactly?

A few days later while back home watching a DVD of Revival teaching by Robert Heidler, I watched as he again mentioned the Waldensians, one of the lights from the Dark Ages; but this time, his PowerPoint showed a map of the Waldensians living in the midst of the French and Italian Alps. Finally, a specific focus! Now onto more targeted research, which pointed to Torre Pellice as our destination town in the Piedmont Region of Northwest Italy, near the border of France.

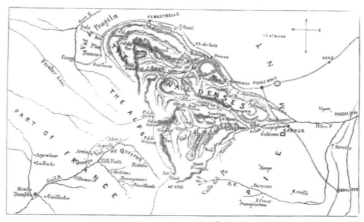

MAP OF THE COUNTRY OF THE WALDENSES.

Once I had that firm internal nod, I ran everything by Linda Heidler, who is the senior leader at Glory of Zion assigned to oversee those of us who are aligned as a Ministry of Zion. She responded that she bore witness to the prayer journey, noting that home base of the Waldensians was the one historical revival location she and her husband Robert had not visited. More research revealed that 29 Waldensians actually founded a town in North Carolina called Valdese. I teamed up with one of our Releasing Heaven Ministries team members and found an open date on our calendars to visit, believing that during our time there the Lord would somehow provide confirmation of our plan regarding the town and other arrangements.

The day we visited the Waldensian Museum and Trail of Faith in Valdese, we met Pat Butler from OM Arts International who just happened to have recently returned from Bobbio Pellice in Italy, a town about 8 kilometers west of Torre Pellice. She also just happened to have a burning passion to find out more about the Waldensians, hoping that the fire that they carried would once again sweep through the church at-large. We were blessed with confirmation on the area to visit, the place to stay ("Forterocca" in Bobbio Pellice, which was also the place that friends of Linda Heidler recommended), and a newfound friend! The volunteer on duty at the exhibit just shook her head as we left, marveling as to how it was possible for us all to just so happen come on the same day.

Who Exactly are the Waldensians?

The Waldensian story varies, depending on the dates and origins of available records of their history. I believe that because they were a heavily persecuted population of believers whose homes and churches were repeatedly destroyed, they lost track of precise places and dates. However, their love of God and their faith never failed them. Since I love history, I will take you back to about 58-59 A.D. During this time, it is believed that some of the early apostles planted the seed of Christianity in their beloved valleys. They are quietly known as the first Christian reformation movement of Europe, but they are not widely recognized as such. Even though at some point they were excommunicated from the then Catholic Church, they never acknowledged any severing of ties with the Church. They are simply a people committed to the Word and to the apostolic doctrines. They believed that everyone should have the right to read the Scriptures for themselves; therefore, they translated the bible into their own language. They also trained ministers and evangelized—all of which was punishable by death per the edict of the Church. They lived in community together and lovingly cared for one another. There is evidence of their having an ancient Confession of Faith of the Waldensians in 1120, which predates Calvin, Luther, and even Peter Waldo.

Peter Waldo (1140-1205) was a wealthy merchant in Lyon, France who had a divine encounter, gave away his wealth, and took up poverty and evangelism. He and other bands of believers were exiled; and they came together in Italy and formed a training center called School of the Barbas. Of course, that was also illegal and punishable by death.

"Lux Lucet in Tenebris" (A Light Shining in the Darkness) is the motto of the Waldensian Community. Their crest shows a lit candle on a bible with seven stars around it. An article found during my research explains, "We are like a lamp that carries the light of the Gospel and we are like the persecuted churches in Revelation 1:16."

Onto Italy—"No Worries, You are Fully Insured"

Our prayer journey to Italy physically began on Tuesday, November 25, 2014. We were now a team of three flying out from Charlotte to Turin via Frankfurt. We had researched and prayed, and our intercessors armed us with various Scripture passages and with prophetic words about angels, divine encounters, and being forever changed. We arrived the next afternoon in Italy, picked up our manual transmission rental car with a GPS that was programmed for English (but with a very heavy Italian accent), and got on our way with a word from the counter agent saying, "No worries, you are fully insured." Those words became our cheer as we made our way from Turin to the Pellice Valley.

Luca and Two Days of "A faith That Is Stronger Than Life"

The next morning in the Town Square of Bobbio Pellice, we meet Luca, our guide from the Waldensian Cultural Center. (We found out later that he is Waldensian and can trace his roots back to the 1450s.) The same heavy fog that had tripled the expected time of our previous night's drive from the airport remained in the morning. As Luca told us of the history of the area, he looked at his new crew, smiled and said that he wanted us to experience what the Waldensians in that town had endured. They were constantly being raided and often resorted to climbing hidden paths up the hillside to secret caves where they had stored food and supplies. Although many were killed, they kept coming back to the land because of their faith in the Word of God and their commitment to honor their Lord and Savior Jesus. They held to Revelation 2:10 (NIV), "do not be afraid of what you are about to suffer. … Be faithful, even to the point of death, and I will give you life as your victor's crown." They also walked in a spirit of forgiveness against those who attacked them. They had "a faith that is stronger than life."

Bobbio Pellice and Monument at Sibaud

At Sibaud, up the hill from the Town Square, was a monument erected in 1889 to commemorate the 200th anniversary of their glorious return from exile. Back in 1689 after years of heavy persecution, the Waldensians went into exile in Switzerland. Yet, they still had no peace because of their commitment to Revelation 2:10. Leaving the older ones and women farther up the mountain, a group of young people, the oldest one being 24, made their way back down to the hill above Bobbio Pellice. They soon found themselves surrounded on all sides, but they dug trenches and worshiped and prayed. A letter written by one young French soldier recorded how he and his fellow soldiers marveled at the faith of these people who sang when they knew they were about to be killed. Lo and behold, a heavy fog settled in over the area, and one young lad remembered a passageway out. Under a blanket of fog, they had escaped. The French soldier's letter also commented on the fog and how they recognized God must have been with these young Waldensians.

Amazed, we thought, wow – my oh my, the fog! During one of our prayer times before leaving on this trip, one of the team members had a vision of fog and colorful ribbons. It represented some aspect of the Glory. Either the Glory was over this area or was to be released over this area. When that vision was released during our prayer time, I saw that the Glory to be released would restore the Song of the Lord over this area. I saw that worship would once again flow down the mountain, over the valley and region. It would flow even to Turin, which had become a center of satanic worship. I had brought along worship ribbon streamers in hopes of doing a prophetic act on the mountains of Italy.

Luca nodded and said that Torre Pellice and Bobbio Pellice have basically the same weather. He stated that the day before it had been clear all day. He said that, yes, the fog there that day was unusual for that time of year.

When we got to the Sibaud monument, we prayed and worshiped for a while, waving those ribbons. We prayed for the remission of sins and the removal of curses brought on by the shedding of innocent blood. We blessed the land and released faith and Glory to continue to hover there.

Torre Pellice, Waldensian Cultural Center, and Links in the Chain

While in the Synod in Torre Pellice, I asked Luca about the varying stories of the origins of the Waldensian faith. He said he believed that the stories are all links in the chain. I asked him specifically about Bishop Claudius of Turin because I found a note about his "being burned at the stake in 839 AD for passionate protests against the Medieval church." Luca responded that the main themes have held true for more than a thousand years: "be faithful, be the prophet, be prayerful." We saw those themes displayed throughout our tour of the Waldensian Cultural Center Museum. Those themes also included a love of the Holy Scriptures, the dedication to and training for evangelism ("the barbas"), and a faith stronger than life amidst an onslaught of violence, murder, and broken covenants.

Angrogna and Rora—The Barbas, The Cave, Chanforan, The Lion, and The Moravians

The Angrogna Valley is home to the Barbas College, which is hidden amongst the homes on the mountainside. The Barbas, meaning "uncles" in their dialect, studied the word there and were discipled in evangelism. They were sent out two by two all across Europe. Angrogna is also the place where over 200 Waldensians who had retreated to a cave were smoked out and slaughtered. But it is also a place of hope. Chanforan in Angrogna is the gathering place where the leaders from all around the region affirmed joining the Reformation. This affirmation came after much prayer (15 years) was released and assurances were received that their statement of faith would not be modified. I was amazed that the Waldensians were not isolationists, and I was proud of the meditative approach they took to joining the movement. According to my research, the Reformation leaders were extremely honored to have the Waldensians, as they were all very impressed and inspired by their faith.

The Rorà Valley was the stage for the resistance of the Waldensians in the persecution and massacre of 1655 called The Spring of Blood. Many Waldensians who would not deny their faith were carried up to the cliffs and thrown into the river below. It was said that the river ran red with blood. One testimony to their "faith that was stronger than life" is the story of one of the leaders of the resistance, Joshua Gianavello (the Lion of Rora). Gianavello was a prosperous farmer and Italian military leader who defended the Waldensians. In an attempt to deter him, the Duke of Savoy kidnapped Gianavello's wife and two daughters and threatened that he would kill them if Gianavello did not renounce his faith and become a Catholic. (The Catholic Church had excommunicated the Waldensians back in the 1100s as they did not practice several of the sacraments: for example, they did not require a priest for the confession of sins and they rejected the use of indulgences.) The Duke finally relented and released his family; and in the meantime, Gianavello became the strategist of the resistance. He even built a tunnel from his home to the cave up the hill as a way of quick escape. Of note is that the Waldensians were trained by him only to defend themselves and never to attack.

We found out just a couple of months prior to this prayer mission trip to Italy that the Moravians were particularly impressed with the faith and stance of the Waldensians. We just happened to have planned a Strategic Prayer Outing to Moravian Falls in North Carolina in September of 2014 and my research for that outing revealed that nine members of The Brethren of the Law of Christ (one of the ancient names of the Moravian Church) were ordained into the ministry by the Waldensians in 1467. The article found on a Moravian Church website revealed that "three of them, Matthias, Thomas, and Elias, were consecrated as bishops. So commenced the line of bishops in our Moravian

Church." Their leader Jan Hus of Bohemia who was a Roman Catholic priest and the President of the University Prague had been martyred in 1415 because he both spoke out against the abuses of the Church including the practice of indulgences and he spoke out for his belief that all Christians had the right and duty to read and interpret the Bible for themselves.

This strong connection between the Waldensians and Moravians brought to mind how Count Zinzendorf and the Moravians, through their Prayer Watch and their mission work, helped birth the First Great Awakening. I then realized three things: one, I spent much of my youth (ages 9-16) connected to a Moravian church in Philadelphia; two, I was living in the town of Bethlehem, Pennsylvania, which Count Zinzendorf founded in 1742, when I had the prophetic night vision in 1990 of apostolic teams of worshipping warriors releasing the anointing for the effective evangelism of towns and villages, neighborhoods and communities; and three, the root of that mission protocol came from the Waldensians and could be traced back to the apostles and how the early church functioned according to Scripture.

Last Day

Early on our final day there, Luca told us that Italy was still only 1% Protestant, and that many in the nation had no real knowledge of the height, depth, and breadth of the truth contained in our beloved Scriptures. Our hearts ached as we ended our time there. We all longed to see the Lord release the blessing of this rich heritage upon all of Italy and the rest of the world.

Nashville and Highway 431

The Altars of the Second Great Awakening—Do It Again, Lord!

During the same visit to Nashville in July 2015 mentioned previously, our friend Dabney told us that near the restaurant where we dined for lunch was the Masonic Lodge that had been the site where President Andrew Jackson's enacted a "treaty" with the Chickasaw Indians (part of the Indian Removal Act of 1830). For several months, my spirit had been burning in righteous anger about the Indian Removal Act; therefore, I asked if we could stop there so that I could add in my prayers of repentance from the Carolinas since both North and South Carolina claimed President Jackson as a native son.

In the midst of our time in front of that lodge, Dabney pointed towards where **Highway 431** ran through Franklin. She spoke of the prophecy about the Lord re-firing the revival that had begun just a short ride away in Kentucky. That fire was best known as the Cane Ridge Revival and the Second Great Awakening; but its spark started about an hour and a half up Highway 431 in Logan County, Kentucky.

James McGready

Immediately my spirit was stirred, but I waited for about a week or so after my return to Charlotte before planning a response while I researched and prayed. During my research, I found a recurring name, James McGready. McGready was born in Pennsylvania and was of Scots-Irish descent. He moved to North Carolina as a youth, felt called to the ministry and was trained in Pennsylvania, but returned to minister in North Carolina. After being run out of town for his fiery preaching, McGready ended up answering a call to pastor three churches in Logan County, Kentucky (Gasper River, Muddy River, and Red River). He arrived in Kentucky in 1796. About a hundred or so other North Carolinians made that journey—some who went before and some who followed. What impressed me the most about McGready were the descriptions I found about his character and his faith in a prayer-hearing God.

Excerpts from The Cumberland Presbyterian archives

These Logan County congregations were small and in a low state of religious interest. There were among them, however, some living and earnest Christians. In addition to working for the conversion of sinners, McGready made great efforts to arouse his people to a proper sense of their spiritual condition. In order to be more effective in reaching his objectives, he presented to the members of his congregation for their approval and signatures, the following preamble and covenant:

"When we consider the word and promises of a compassionate God to the poor lost family of Adam, we find the strongest encouragement for Christians to pray in faith–to ask in the name of Jesus for the conversion of their fellow-men. None ever went to Christ when on earth, with the case of their friends, that were denied, and, although the days of his humiliation are ended, yet, for the encouragement of his people, he has left it on record, that where two or three agree upon earth to ask in prayer, *believing*, it shall be done. Again, whatsoever you shall ask the Father in my name, that will I do, that the Father may be glorified in the Son. With these promises before us, we feel encouraged to unite our supplications to a prayer-hearing God for the outpouring of his Spirit, that his people may be quickened and comforted, and that our children, and sinners generally, may be converted. Therefore, we bind ourselves to observe the third Saturday of each month, for one year, as a day of fasting and prayer for the conversion of sinners in Logan County, and throughout the world. We also engage to spend one half hour every Saturday evening, beginning at the setting of the sun, and one half hour every Sabbath morning, from the rising of the sun, pleading with God to revive his work."

To this covenant, he and they affixed their names.

Logan County to Cane Ridge, Kentucky

As I prayed over all that I had discovered, I knew Holy Spirit was sending us on a prayer assignment. Our main targets were going through Nashville, visiting Logan County, driving down Highway 431, and hopefully being able to stretch ourselves to include Cane Ridge Meeting House in Paris, Kentucky. (We later found out that at her founding as a city, Nashville was a part of the state of North Carolina.)

On our way!

We actually started our journey at Cane Ridge Meeting House. During our 4-hour drive from Nashville to Cane Ridge, we shared some of the research, listened to revival messages from various leaders, and prayed for an awakening of our nation. Our cry was "Lord, send the revival fire from the Second Great Awakening to our nation once again. We are lost without you. Our nation, once again, is full of lawlessness and our hearts have grown cold again. We need you, Lord. Only you can save us. Do it again, Lord!"

Cane Ridge Meeting House

Upon our arrival at Cane Ridge Meeting House, we were graciously greeted by the curator, who shared the history of Cane Ridge with us. His talk, although dotted with doubt and unbelief, was filled with the reality that 25,000 people gathered on this high place for a solid week back in August 1801. They brought their cows and chickens. There were soldiers stationed nearby who helped cart water to what had become campgrounds. The Lord indeed showed up. Even in the first three days of rain, people were slain in the spirit ("the falling exercise") and literally rolled in the mud under the power of God. Although there was a mocking undertone from the curator, our hearts were filled with rejoicing to hear about this outpouring of Holy Spirit. The revival ended only because they ran out of food. We cried out in our hearts for the Lord to do it again and that it would be unending.

About that time, a prayer group from a local church arrived. The curator had mentioned in an email exchange earlier that week that they may be meeting there from 3:00-5:00 pm that day. I quietly hoped that we would be like-minded enough to connect, even for a short while; but if not, we planned to just walk the grounds during that time. Needless to say, we were thrilled when the prayer group invited us to join them. They were a spirit-filled group who, likewise, were there to stoke the fire for another Great Awakening. Their leader had gotten held up in traffic but when he arrived, he added in a CD of wonderful worship music that we gratefully were familiar with. We even prayed for Israel; and at the end, their leader anointed us with oil from the Land. Hallelujah!

Logan County, Kentucky

We stayed overnight in Lexington and started out the next morning to head to Logan County where the three river churches that James McGready pastored were located. Cane Ridge has received most of the notoriety as one of the key sparks of the Second Great Awakening because their camp meetings swelled to 25,000 attendees. Those numbers at Cane Ridge were truly a sign, because that part of the country was mainly farmland. *(And of course in 1801, they did not have all of our modern communication methods, such as phones and the internet, to let people know about the camp meetings; but that news somehow spread.)*

However, the Second Great Awakening actually began at the small congregations in Logan County, where the membership was 20-35 people in each location. Logan County was the western frontier at that time, and truly the wild, wild west. It was called the Rogue Harbor as it was a hiding place for outlaws and bandits. The nation itself was in a very hard place of apostasy. Ideas such as Thomas Paine's The Age of Reason were circulating from the French Revolution. In addition, people had been hardened by the American Revolutionary war. Their hearts and minds were generally very far from thinking about the Lord.

South Union and Russellville, Kentucky

Our goals upon crossing into Logan County were to find places close enough to where Gasper River and Muddy River Meeting Houses used to be and also to travel from Russellville, the county seat, down Highway 431 to the Red River Meeting House to pray. Off we went, riding across Kentucky to reach Highway 68, which runs East and West across Logan County. It was a two and a half hour journey, so we also prayed as we drove.

It was early Sunday morning when we reached South Union and the Shaker Village; therefore, we prayed where we briefly stopped. The Gasper River Meeting House was reported to have been just a few miles from there. We then headed to the town square in Russellville as another touch point and prayed there. The Muddy River Meeting House was reported to have been five miles north.

Down Highway 431

Then we headed down Highway 431 to the Red River Meeting House and continued reading our research and praying. There were various reports as to where the revival actually started and which leader it could be attributed to; but the thing that I loved is that these reports all came from various denominations – Methodist, Presbyterian, Baptist. This movement of God was ecumenical and impacted men and women, young and old alike. I recommend that you do an internet search to find the personal account of Elder Reuben Ross that details the outpouring that happened at the Red River Meeting House.

Red River Meeting House

When you first arrive at the Meeting House site, you will find a cemetery. There are flyers describing its history along with a rock memorial marking where the original site was located. One of the things that struck me that Releasing Heaven Ministries teammate Doris read from the flyer was that they had gathered here to pray for the restoration of the Christian heritage of this nation. After spending time outside reading the history and praying, we entered the Meeting House. We opened all of the windows and sat down on the benches. Doris led us in a couple of songs to welcome the Lord's presence. Then we prayed and travailed for the awakening that we knew we were entering, but we cried out for the fullness – "Do it again, Lord!"

Portions of Psalm 91 were read from the pulpit as we continued to cry out to the Lord. We ended our time there with communion, which was the very reason they had gathered together on that day back in June 1800. As we left, we saw a bonfire outside, ready to be lit. We again cried out, "O Lord, yes, do it again!"

Highway 431 Prophecy and the Angel of Revival

When I returned home, I found a YouTube video of Ken Malone and a group worshiping the Lord in the Red River Meeting House. Back in 2010, after hearing about a prophetic word from Ray Hughes that "There will be a move of God-doin's on Highway 431," Ken received an unction from Holy Spirit to do an Awakening Tour along Highway 431. Holy Spirit had spoken to Ken and said, "This is an Acts 4:31 highway." He wrote that, as he pondered the prophetic word given by Holy Spirit over the next several days, he felt the Lord's Presence beside him, and then he heard, "The angel of Revival is with you now."

Acts 4:31 (NASB) reads, "And when they had prayed, the place where they had gathered together was shaken, and they were all filled with the Holy Spirit, and began to speak the word of God with boldness."

Impact of the Second Great Awakening

The effects of the Second Great Awakening with its small beginnings could indeed be felt throughout our nation. The impact not only spanned distance, it spanned time. On October 10, 1821, Charles Finney, a young lawyer in upstate New York, walked into the woods near his home to have an encounter with God. He said, "I will give my heart to God, or I never will come down from there." After several hours, he returned to his office, where he experienced such forceful emotion that he questioned those who could not testify to a similar encounter. "The Holy Spirit … seemed to go through me, body, and soul," he later wrote. "I could feel the impression, like a wave of electricity, going through and through me. Indeed it seemed to come in waves of liquid love, for I could not express it in any other way." The next morning, Finney returned to his law office to meet with a client whose case he was about to argue. "I have a retainer from the Lord Jesus Christ to plead his cause," he told the man, "and cannot plead yours."

Finney's ministry so transformed an entire region such that it became known as the "burned over district." The city of Rochester, New York was particularly impacted and changed. Social reform also came out of this wave of revival. Finney himself was a strong abolitionist, and he encouraged Christians to become involved in the antislavery movement. Christians became the leaders in many other social concerns, such as education, prison reform, temperance, Sabbath observance, and women's rights. The large numbers of Christian workers for social reform became so influential that they and the organizations they founded became known as the Benevolent Empire. It has been reported that the Second Great Awakening had a greater effect on society than any other revival in America.

We Say, "Yes Lord, Do It Again!"

Rev. Robert Hunt— Can These Dry Bones Live?

Dry bones and the Covenant Root in Virginia

In 2015 while planning a Thanksgiving getaway, I felt a quickening about visiting Virginia Beach. As I mentioned in an earlier chapter, eight years prior in 2007, having arrived early in Virginia Beach for a prophetic conference, I met a local pastor who told me about Rev. Robert Hunt and about both the cross he planted and the prayer of dedication he made in 1607 at what is now known as the First Landing. Neither at that time nor for several years after that was I able to actually visit the First Landing site. Then in July 2015, I read that they had finally positively identified a set of bones that they had excavated in Jamestown a couple years prior as those of Rev. Robert Hunt. My spirit was stirred as I thought it was a profound and much needed sign for this nation to remember her history, her root of covenant, her prophetic destiny!

The synergy of the ages

I felt burdened to walk that First Landing Beach, find the spot where the cross was planted, repent there on behalf of the nation for our sin of falling away from the Lord, and rededicate her to the Lord. I would also ask the Lord to visit us again. I could almost hear Dutch Sheets' voice resounding in my ear, "it is the synergy of the ages – we need to step into the timeline of the old, old stories."

Confirmation and Isaiah 22:22

I planned to get re-fired before my departure to Virginia Beach since Dutch was speaking at Glory of Zion the weekend prior to Thanksgiving at the Awakening Our Prophetic Destiny for the

Future Conference. However, the communication lines in the region had been severed, and I was unable to receive any live feed. I drove the six hours there on Sunday and got settled in. It wasn't until the early hours of Monday morning that I caught Dutch's message from Friday night. Dutch spoke of the keys of opening doors no man could shut and closing doors no man could open (Isaiah 22:22). He also spoke of the high-level assignments of apostolic and prophetic intercession being given out to the <u>ekklesia</u> (the Greek word for church or assembly, literally meaning the called-out ones). Dutch proclaimed, "He's going to send us on high level assignments. He's going to shift nations and governments in this season through apostolic intercession. Not just through apostles, but through apostolic and prophetic intercession. ...This move of the Spirit that's coming and the prayer movement that's coming is not for the chosen few. It's for the available few. There are going to be people sent to palaces that nobody will ever know they've been there, and it will shift the government over a nation." Chuck then prophesied about a shift happening, going back to the covenantal roots in Virginia. And here I was—*in Virginia!*

Apostolic and Prophetic Decrees

My, my. I knew that I was in the right place at the right time. I knew what I needed to do. I had to make decrees based on Isaiah 22:22 and somehow plant a key when I went to the cross that Friday.

My Prayer at the Cross

On that Friday, I rose early and went through the checkpoint at Fort Story. I spent an hour in worship and prayer and completed my assignment.

HERE AT CAPE HENRY FIRST LANDED IN
AMERICA UPON 26 APRIL 1607 THOSE
ENGLISH COLONISTS WHO, UPON 13 MAY 1607,
ESTABLISHED AT JAMESTOWN, VIRGINIA, THE
FIRST PERMANENT ENGLISH SETTLEMENT
IN AMERICA

ERECTED BY
NATIONAL SOCIETY DAUGHTERS
OF THE AMERICAN COLONISTS
APRIL 26, 1935

In the months prior to my trip, I was able to watch the webcast of Glory of Zion's Head of the Year 5776 Conference held in September and several of their Sunday Celebration services. So I had my spirit full of prophetic revelation and decrees from other trusted leaders which I also was able to carry with me to Virginia Beach. At the Head of the Year Conference, Robert Heidler had shared on the prophetic meaning of the new year on God's calendar, 5776. The 76 in Hebrew is <u>Ayin</u> (70) <u>Vav</u> (6). <u>Ayin</u> again means "eye," so we are in the decade when God wants to give us clear vision to see what we could not see before. A <u>vav</u> is a picture of a connecting pin that holds things together and joins things. Robert taught that the first use of <u>vav</u> in the Bible is Genesis 1:1, "In the beginning God created the heavens and earth." He explained that Jews picture a single beam of light from God's infinite source shining into the universe and heaven invading earth. In addition to vav being a year for heaven to invade earth, he further taught that it also is a year that the Lord is connecting our past with our present. Then on Sunday, November 14th, Chuck prophesied: "We are in war. Without the restraining force of Holy Spirit being present, the enemy has access."

I decreed at the cross, "In this year of <u>Ayin</u> <u>Vav</u> and at the beginnings of the second phase of the Third Great Awakening, I stand at the foot of the cross that is a granite replica of the one planted by Robert Hunt on 29 April 1607, where he dedicated this nation to the Lord Jesus Christ and to the preaching of the gospel to all inhabitants here and also to all nations, and with the prophetic sign of the recent identification of his bones, I stake that original covenant to the current and future destiny of our nation and I rededicate the United States of America to the Lord Jesus Christ and to the purposes of preaching the gospel and advancing His Kingdom (Isaiah 22:22)."

I then went to First Landing Beach and knelt there also and prayed. Finally, I journeyed to the Jamestown Settlement site to walk and pray in the spirit.

There's Power in the Bones!

It was not until almost a week later that I heard Dutch's Saturday message, which talked about Robert Hunt's bones! Holy Spirit was speaking. I can tell you that something shifted in my spirit while "on assignment" in Virginia Beach. – I felt Holy Spirit fire in my bones once again! I felt the resonance of the roar of the Lion of the Tribe of Judah through my core—and there was a listening, watching, and waiting for more assignments.

Excerpts from the Saturday morning session at Glory of Zion's Awakening Our Prophetic Destiny Conference:

James sings: "Some of us thought we had seen the finalization of some things. Some of us saw even death and destruction and we thought it was over. We thought whatever prayers and whatever we had released had been finalized and perhaps the answer that happened was not the answer we were looking for. And that it was over. But just as the man was thrown onto the bones of Elisha and he was raised up from the dead, the Lord says the power of those prayers, the power of your answer is still within me. And although it seems a door had shut, the open door is in me. The answer is in me. And you will see it come around in another way. … The time has come back around. Life is coming round again. There's power in the bones. There's still power in the bones. There's still power in the bones. The time is now. The time is now. The time is now. The time is now. The time is now. There's power in the prayers, there's power in the bones, the time is now. There's power in the prayers, there's power in the bones, the time is now."

Chuck: "This is a word from the Lord. There's power in the bones—it is where the word of God dwells. … The word of God is quick and powerful, sharper than any two-edged sword, piercing, dividing soul and spirit going even down into your bone marrow."

Dutch: "As I went back through the history of awakening— I pondered what are the verses that are important to us? What should we agree with? What do you want me to grab? I've studied our history. Let me tell you what I think God's purpose for America is. 1607 they planted a cross and dedicated this land to the glory of God. They found four skeletons at Jamestown – one is Robert Hunt's skeleton. Don't miss that – in this season, it is a sign to us."

My spirit cried out —at the scent of water! Job 14: 7-9 (NASB): "For there is hope for a tree, When it is cut down, that it will sprout again, And its shoots will not fail. Though its roots grow old in the ground And its stump dies in the dry soil, At the scent of water it will flourish And put forth sprigs like a plant."

Guilford County, North Carolina—Preparing a Place for an Outpouring

In 2016, Releasing Heaven Ministries was asked to do some training for another ministry in Guilford County. The Lord had us do our usual research, but He also had us send out a small advance team to put "boots on the ground" for some spiritual recon. What we found was that we could sense the Lord's Presence hovering over the Guilford Courthouse National Military Park.

We completed the training; then to seal our time in that county, we planned a follow-up Strategic Prayer Outing. We found out that a re-enactment of the Battle of Guilford Courthouse was occurring on March 12, so we gathered our troops and headed that way.

Training Recap: The Power of Worship and Prayer, The Power of Covenant, The Power of Prophetic Destiny and Redemptive Purpose

For the training, we shared through Scripture and testimonies about the power of Worship and Prayer, including engaging angelic help. We also shared about the Covenants of God including the covenant with Israel into which we were grafted. Additionally, we shared America's Christian heritage and her prophetic destiny. We taught on strategic prayer through spiritual mapping and putting "boots on the ground."

There were folks from other states there, and we decided to activate the participants by dividing them into teams wherein we could help them formulate an initial apostolic and prophetic prayer strategy for their state. Finally, we helped them execute that strategy through Watchman-style worship and prayer. We spoke into each state's redemptive purpose and stood against the demonic strongholds through repentant hearts and the use of our arsenal of the Word of God, prophetic decrees, and praying in the Spirit.

Battle of Guilford Courthouse

On March 12, we stepped onto the battlefield as we heard the re-enactment guns go off in the distance. After "gathering more intel" at the Visitor Center and Museum, we found a clearing nearby where we could prayerfully enter into the prophetic atmosphere that had been set-up for us.

I started our prayer time by submitting my impressions of the day. I recounted that as I walked through the Visitor Center's exhibits, I was once again overwhelmed with the evidence of how the Lord most assuredly was with America's army as she battled, for a very grueling eight long years, an army that was far better-equipped and far better-trained. I also confessed my admiration for Nathanael Greene, who was an untrained, relatively very young Quaker with what had to be a supernatural gift of wisdom. General Greene led a hodge-podge company of soldiers with widely varying skill levels and was able to devise strategically brilliant war plans. I also marveled at how both the Quakers and the Moravians just so happened to have settled in this region, as I knew the power of their faith and prayer life.

In that moment, I could feel the Lord's heart for His blood-bought but heavily persecuted church. I had a sense of knowing about how mightily He would move heaven and earth to restore her to the fullness of His glory. I could feel, in spite of the oft-times tragic missteps and hardships created by slavery and the displacement of the Native Americans, that the Lord was establishing a place where the fullness of His Spirit could come forth in such a way as to touch the whole world and redeem all. In my spirit, I could almost hear the sounds and sense the activity from the moments of Rev. Robert Hunt's prayers as he dedicated this nation to the Lord with the proclamation that the gospel would go forth from these shores, to the tarrying songs and prayers that stirred the fire that fell on Azusa Street, which ushered over 600 million spirit-filled souls into the kingdom. I could hear the same drums that had been sounded on this battlefield echoing out a call to the next generation who were at the various colleges in the "hillside round about."

Subsequently we released a warring sound as we called out to the next generation to take their places as we made pledges to run with them. We cried out to the Lord for a fresh outpouring of His wartime strategies! We decreed that the Church's enemies would once again be thwarted as we got in position to see the fullness of our splendor manifest like that of Queen Esther—for such a time as this! We invoked the covenant and ordained destiny of our nation as well as the open portal for national transformation that still hovered over Greensboro (Guilford County) to cry out for a resettling of our nation on Godly, Christian, ethical, and righteous foundations.

Isaiah 32: 1-8, 14-20 (NIV), See, a king will reign in righteousness and rulers will rule with justice. Each one will be like a shelter from the wind and a refuge from the storm, like streams of water in the desert and the shadow of a great rock in a thirsty land. Then the eyes of those who see will no longer be closed, and the ears of those who hear will listen. The fearful heart will know and understand, and the stammering tongue will be fluent and clear. No longer will the fool be called noble nor the scoundrel be highly respected. For fools speak folly, their hearts are bent on evil: They practice ungodliness and spread error concerning the LORD; the hungry they leave empty and from the thirsty they withhold water. Scoundrels use wicked methods, they make up evil schemes to destroy the poor with lies, even when the plea of the needy is just. But the noble make noble plans, and by noble deeds they stand. … The fortress will be abandoned, the noisy city deserted; citadel and watchtower will become a wasteland forever, the delight of donkeys, a pasture for flocks, till the Spirit is poured on us from on high, and the desert becomes a fertile field, and the fertile field seems like a forest. The LORD's justice will dwell in the desert, his righteousness live in the fertile field. The fruit of that righteousness will be peace; its effect will be quietness and confidence forever. My people will live in peaceful dwelling places, in secure homes, in undisturbed places of rest. Though hail flattens the forest and the city is leveled completely, how blessed you will be, sowing your seed by every stream, and letting your cattle and donkeys range free.

The Lord's Military Strategies—Repairing the Breaches and Stretching Your Tent Curtains Wide

Repairing the Breaches—Angelic Help and Two Proclamations

At the founding of Releasing Heaven Ministries (RHM), the Lord reaffirmed that I was not to move to Texas as He had "called me to The Carolinas." I remember seeing the landscape of our region in dreams and visions back in 1996. My family is originally from both states; my mother's side is primarily from a small town called Manson in North Carolina, and my dad was born in Denmark, South Carolina.

YVONNE DENISE

Although Releasing Heaven Ministries is organized in North Carolina's jurisdiction, we have always seen the territory assigned to us by the Lord for us to watch over as including both states and their bordering states. It was interesting that at our commissioning as a Ministry of Zion, Anne Tate prophesied about our being a new order of Watchmen over South Carolina. As Chuck Pierce and C. Peter Wagner wrapped the Elijah prayer shawl that I had purchased for this occasion around Releasing Heaven Ministries teammate Rosemerry and me, Chuck further prophesied that it was a mantle for quick expansion. We were to pinpoint our location and go North, South, East and West.

Prior to my actual commissioning as a Ministry of Zion, my first ministry activity, after all of our organizing paperwork was submitted to North Carolina's Secretary of State, was a week of rest to pray and to hear further instructions from the Lord. The beach is one of my favorite places for that level of contemplative prayer, as I feel like I can almost touch the hem of heaven's garment when I gaze out over the water. So in December 2012, I journeyed with another intercessor to Hilton Head Island in Beaufort County, South Carolina to do just that. There I had an open vision of Harriet Tubman. That encounter is one of my Isaiah 46:10 (NIV) moments that Dutch Sheets often emphasizes: "I make known the end from the beginning, from ancient times, what is still to come. I say, 'My purpose will stand, and I will do all that I please.'" I will share more about that encounter at the end of this chapter.

To date, we have ministered in several counties of South Carolina including Charleston, Edgefield, Beaufort, Greenville and York counties, and we have prayer-walked the University of South Carolina campus in Columbia. I will highlight in the pages that follow the times where I have had the most profound angelic and prophetic encounters tied to the two major breaches in the history of the Carolinas: the split of the Carolinas into two colonies, and the Civil War. South Carolina was the first state to secede from the Union, and North Carolina was the last. Both of

132

these breaches formed iniquitous structures in our territory as they in essence were the breaking of a covenant. (Galatians 3:15, ESV: To give a human example, brothers, even with a man-made covenant, no one annuls it or adds to it once it has been ratified.)

Charleston: The Wind of Healing

In March 2014, a small group of mighty prayer warriors were prompted by Holy Spirit to begin prayer-walking their city, so they asked our ministry for some help. In response, we sent a small team to do training and activation. For training, we met at a local church to worship, pray, and teach; and we planned an outing the next day at The Battery in Downtown Charleston. During our prayer time, Holy Spirit showed me that there was still a spirit of arrogance in the atmosphere that had originated in the posture of several, but not all, of the founders of the Carolinas. Many lived for themselves, and many of the broken covenants, and even the secession back in 1860, was due to their wanting to maintain their lifestyle. This arrogance was like idolatry before the Lord. The attendees concurred. 1 Samuel 15:23 NIV: "For rebellion is like the sin of divination, and arrogance like the evil of idolatry."

At The Battery, the joint team entered into a time of worship and a time of repentance. The Battery is now one of the major tourist attractions in Charleston located at the base of the convergence of the Ashley and Cooper Rivers with scenic views of historic Fort Sumter, the historic promenade of colorful antebellum homes, and White Point Garden. Its history includes being an artillery battery in both the Revolutionary and Civil Wars. And its location is said to have given residents a front row seat to the first shot and ensuing first battle of the Civil War.

We decreed from there, as we know many other believers in that city had, that Jesus was Lord over Charleston. We welcomed Holy Spirit and the hosts of heaven and cried out for an awakening! We also sought the Lord to stir His people to venture out and use their giftings to draw the lost unto Him; His Kingdom come, His will be done!

On our return trip home to Charlotte, the team met heavy winds, the keep-two-hands-on-the-wheel kind. Later, we found out that during Glory of Zion's Aligning the Armies of Heaven Conference, held that same weekend, James Goll and Tim Sheets were teaching about how the angels come on the wind! So, we decreed that there was a breakthrough, with more "help" being sent to Charleston and to the rest of the Carolinas.

We have ventured back to the Charleston area on a few more occasions: to prayer-walk the colleges in November 2014, to help heal the land after the tragic shooting at the Emanuel AME Church in June 2015, and to gather some of God's Kingdom Women for encouragement and refreshing in November 2017. An answer to these decrees, as well as the ones made in the other counties as highlighted below, has been the series of meetings that Chuck Pierce and Dutch Sheets have done in the Carolinas since 2017. Later in this chapter I share two of the proclamations they led our region in.

Edgefield: Stepping under the Open Heaven for a Glory Shift in our territory!

An earthquake occurred late in the evening of February 14, 2014. It was the night of the homegoing of Bob Jones, a major prophet who lived in our region. The Lord promised Bob that before he would go home he would see the beginning of the harvest of a billion souls into the kingdom. The epicenter of that earthquake was in Edgefield, South Carolina.

We planned an outing there in May 2014 in order that, for our territory, we could step into the open heaven as prophesied. Here are some of the confirming prophetic words from Glory of Zion about the shaking that the Lord had started:

Chuck: "I say to you this is not the same as you've seen in the past. This is not the same of what you've asked for in other seasons. I say this is a different glory, a glory change that I'm bringing into the land. I say you will shudder at the changes that are on the way in your land and in other lands and with other people. For this is a time that the blood that runs deep will now be sanctified. This is a time that my Spirit will go deeper than I have gone in the past, for this is a time of birthing what is new, and yet bringing forth that which is old. And treasures will erupt. Treasures will erupt. Treasures will erupt. I say to you I will bring forth what has not been seen and I will cause your gifts to come alive in ways they've never come alive. So, I say you will feel the shuddering birthing pains within you, and from that you will bring forth the change that is necessary for you to enter in to this season. ...And the shakings of the land are a sign for what will come forth. For the land must give up what is held back in days ahead. And the voice that's been captured in the land, I say, will arise and be satisfied…" (March 30, 2014)

Chuck: "For you have been limited in earthly service. You have been limited and underneath that which is ruling in the atmosphere over you. But this day, and this Passover, I am beginning to remove the limitations that have been on My people in their earthly service to Me. I am going to send an awakening shake to the last religious structure that will cause the earthly service of limitation to be lifted. When you feel the lifting, when you feel the shake underneath you, know that the atmosphere over you is now lifting. The earthly service of My people is now going to be liberated. What is coming from heaven now will create a manifestation. We are going to start seeing certain earthquakes happen … You need to know that means there is an open heaven over that territory, and God is shaking down the old structures that are stopping the next move of God. I then heard the Spirit of God say, 'Do not look and view from the earth. View what I am doing from your seat in heaven that I have prepared for you.'"(April 18, 2014)

135

During our outing, as we crossed into the county of Edgefield, there was an atmosphere and scenery shift. There was a sense of great joy as the landscapes we began to pass were green pastures. We were excited to be on the journey to this small county that had somehow brought forth ten of the State's governors and had reportedly experienced such a history of violence that not one square foot of its town square was without bloodshed.

Upon arrival, we landed in the town square that looked like a snapshot out of time. We gathered with our prayer weapons of bibles, a shofar, a bell, and a rod, and we preceded to repent of past iniquities including lawlessness, pandemonium, and unjust scales that came through the slave trade and Indian warfare. We prayed a fresh release of the Blood of Jesus to wash away all sin and iniquity. And we loosed kingdom rule such that the warrior spirit in the land would be brought under the authority of Holy Spirit. We later walked the land around the square and loosed a release from its history of violence and secessionism as there were statues and plaques all around the square celebrating those stories. (Note that the governor at the time of South Carolina's secession during the Civil War was from Edgefield, and certain battles between the Union and Confederate armies were fought right in the town square.)

We also released some of the treasures of blessings that were in the land. There was an anointing in the land to accumulate great wealth and there was a camaraderie amongst the races. For example, after the Civil War, a freed slave formed a network of over 40 churches in Edgefield and Aiken Counties. Also, Dr. Benjamin Mays, who was president of Morehouse College in Atlanta and mentor to many (including Dr. Martin Luther King, Jr., and Dr. Charles Gomillion, educator and lead plaintiff in a landmark Civil Rights voting case) was amongst some of the prominent citizens of Edgefield County.

York County: Warring at The Gateway to South Carolina

In 2016, I asked a friend living in the area to recommend a place to pray in Rock Hill, which is the largest city in York County and is nicknamed The Gateway to South Carolina. She suggested Winthrop University. After seeking the Lord, that bore witness to my spirit, so we proceeded.

The Little Chapel on Founders Lane

Once on campus, our first stop was The Little Chapel on Founders Lane, which was originally built in 1823. The Little Chapel was first designed and built as the stable and carriage house for a mansion in downtown Columbia. That mansion was purchased in 1830 by the Presbyterian Synod for the Columbia Theological Seminary. Then in 1886, while the Seminary was closed due to a religious dispute, the founder of Winthrop requested to use it as its first classroom for the inaugural year of its training school for women teachers. However, it was used as such for only one year. Then many years later, in 1927, after the chapel had been abandoned, the college petitioned to move it from Columbia to Rock Hill, and did so brick by brick. The chapel was so significant to the school that its founder and his wife are both interred there.

Stepping into history and into war

Not only had the chapel been surrounded by dissension, but South Carolina herself has a long history of war and division. From the period of the Spanish conquistadors, early explorers who left a trail of brutal acts, to even modern times, the land has been overshadowed by pride, greed, and contentions. There were Indian wars: the native Catawbas, for example, although friendly to the settlers, often warred with the other surrounding Indian nations. There were also the horrors that came with the enslavement of

African people, as well as the tension leading to the splitting of the colony once known simply as Carolina into North and South. And in the midst of it all, the Scots-Irish Presbyterians also settled in the York County area, after first fleeing religious persecution in Europe and then high prices in the North.

The American Revolutionary War also brought fierce battles to the York County area, including the one on Kings Mountain that is said to have turned the tide towards victory. And then there was the Civil War—as I previously noted, South Carolina was the first to secede; and Charleston was the city where the first shot of the war rang out. Just a few months after our prayer time here, I specifically journeyed to Charleston to visit Fort Sumter, which took that first shot. While walking through the Fort, I realized that not much was said about where the shot came from. I did some quick research to find out where the remains of Fort Johnson were located, and then I went there to walk the grounds and release prayers of repentance.

Issuing another decree

Moreover, South Carolina is one of two states with no recognition of the Lord in its constitution. Since I had moved to Charlotte, I always sensed an atmosphere of poverty and oppression over her. BUT we issued another decree for her, agreeing with the prayers released by Dutch Sheets, Chuck Pierce and others as recorded in their book <u>Releasing the Prophetic Destiny of a Nation</u>, as well as with the prayers of those of the many thriving churches and ministries that call South Carolina home:

- "Instead of secession, South Carolina will lead in intercession"– in recent years, they removed the Confederate flag from their capitol building;

- "You are a gatekeeper and doorkeeper for the Lord;"

- "You are going to move with Me and liberty will come from South Carolina."

Distractions, Knighted Angels and Coronation

Our live worship time, however, had several interesting challenges. We were fighting through sicknesses on the team, and there were several very unusual distractions. It lasted the entire time, and we worshiped for three solid hours.

Even still, our worship was breaking through in the midst of what felt like a whirlwind; even a few students who drifted in were being blessed. Plus, I could feel the presence of knighted angels. I had been seeing them out of the corner of my eyes for several weeks. I asked the team to meditate about our new angelic company, and I also sought the Lord for several days both alone and with some of our senior leaders about the fine-tuning we obviously needed to do regarding our prayer outreaches. I could sense that the season had changed.

There were several positive strategic outcomes: first, confirmation about angels in battle gear was found on page 244 of Chuck's book <u>A Time to Triumph</u>—one of the Glory of Zion team members had seen them in one of her dreams; second, as I had mentioned in the Introduction, during the Ephesians4Movement (E4M) Equipping service that following Sunday, the Lord walked into our meeting room with more knighted angels and presented me with a crown —it was an official coronation that was both personal and corporate—our warring thrust us into a new mantle of favor and authority; third, there were many leaders in the Body of Christ who testified that the Lord had them reassess their strategies and alignments so that they could be more fully equipped, empowered, and in the right position for the season ahead.

I recently asked the Lord again about the knighted angels; and the impression I received was that some of these angels were actually wearing some of our armor. Personally I have sensed that there are a number of people in the Body of Christ who either have not been trained in spiritual warfare or they have laid down their armor and weapons. I also believe that some of the armor and weapons are an upgrade for the new war and new battles that we have entered in. I recommend three of Chuck's books for equipping: <u>The Future War of the Church</u>, <u>God's Unfolding Battle Plan</u>, and <u>The Spiritual Warfare Handbook</u>.

Ephesians 6: 10-18 (NIV): Finally, be strong in the Lord and in his mighty power. Put on the full armor of God, so that you can take your stand against the devil's schemes. For our struggle is not against flesh and blood, but against the rulers, against the authorities, against the powers of this dark world and against the spiritual forces of evil in the heavenly realms. Therefore put on the full armor of God, so that when the day of evil comes, you may be able to stand your ground, and after you have done everything, to stand. Stand firm then, with the belt of truth buckled around your waist, with the breastplate of righteousness in place, and with your feet fitted with the readiness that comes from the gospel of peace. In addition to all this, take up the shield of faith, with which you can extinguish all the flaming arrows of the evil one. Take the helmet of salvation and the sword of the Spirit, which is the word of God. And pray in the Spirit on all occasions with all kinds of prayers and requests. With this in mind, be alert and always keep on praying for all the Lord's people.

Chuck and Dutch in the Carolinas—
Releasing Proclamations

From September 2017 through March 2019, Chuck and Dutch have come to the Carolinas three times. Prior to that, Chuck commissioned John and Sheryl Price from New Jersey to lead a 13 Colony prayer movement. They came to the Carolinas in July 2017, two months prior to their Unlocking the Wind and Voice Gathering. Releasing Heaven Ministries was blessed to be invited to participate by Anne and Susie of Embassy of Zion, another House of Zion in Charlotte. The group that they assembled were able to pray at key historic sites in Uptown Charlotte. We started out at the statue of Captain Jack, the rider who took the Mecklenburg Declaration of Independence to the Philadelphia Convention in 1775. The site was also a part of the Thompson Orphanage founded in the late 1800s. As prayers were being offered up to come against the orphan spirit in our city, some of our community currently homeless joined us. Thus, we were able to activate our prayers by ministering to them. Then, at Polk Park, named after one of Charlotte's earliest settlers and located at the intersection of two of the original Native American trade paths, we prayed about the City's prosperity. As a part of those prayers, we tapped into our city's gold mining history—there are still gold mine veins that lie underneath Uptown. Gold is connected prophetically with the glory of the Lord's Presence. I mentioned that our football stadium nearby is surrounded by gold mine veins. That stadium has been at the center of a prophecy about revival for our region, and it was dedicated by Billy Graham for the glory of God in August 1996. About a month later, Billy held a four-day crusade there that drew over 330,000 people. We finished our prayer walk at the Settlers' Cemetery. We prayed there with thanksgiving about those who sacrificed their lives for our future generations, and we loosed decrees to establish and safeguard the future of our youth and young adults.

When Chuck and Dutch came that September, one of the key themes was about releasing The Wind—a new prophetic mantle filled with Holy Spirit and led by Holy Spirit. Chuck prophesied out of Ezekiel 37 about the roar of Holy Spirit coming through the Carolinas. Then Dutch released The Voice of the Lord —His Voice to create, to birth, to resurrect, to bring direction, and to judge His enemies. The Wind and The Voice crowning, realigning—breaking down race and class structures, accelerating and releasing the double portion mantle of anointing for harvest and evangelism from this place to the ends of the earth. Both of them also gave confirming words about colleges and universities in our region. Just a few days prior to this gathering, our ministry prayer-walked the campus of the University of North Carolina at Greensboro. While standing in front of their gym, I saw a vision of revival breaking out. It looked like a modern version of historic revival tent meetings.

In October 2018, Chuck and Dutch released powerful words during their Double Portion of Harvest Glory in The Carolinas Gathering. One of those words contained a decree that The Carolinas (both North and South as one, along with the covenant root in Virginia) would become The New Gate to our nation. We stepped into that proclamation more fully when they returned in March 2019 for their gathering called A Time to Plow: Preparing the Land for Awakening! The gathering was held in Columbia, the capital of South Carolina. There was an incredible new sound released that night—it was triumphantly glorious! The Lord had given Chuck a word at least 18 years prior about what transpired during that gathering. Chuck mentioned that one of the confirming signs the Lord gave him to watch for was the removal of the confederate flag from the South Carolina State House Grounds. So Chuck and Dutch's assignment this time was to lead us in repentance over the marriage of religion and politics—South Carolina voted to secede from the Union at the First Baptist Church in Columbia. And then they stirred the fire for restoration, even to the restoration of the Lord's original intent for the Carolinas. That restoration was tied to the treasury; this was profound for me in reflecting back on the gold coins the Lord emphasized during my 2013 trip to Philadelphia. It also seemed linked to the open vision the Lord gave me at the beginning of January 2018 of angels blowing trumpets over and into Uptown Charlotte. I will share on that further in the next chapter.

There was a proclamation of a new covering coming down over America as we worshiped. Dutch had relayed the prophetic decree the Lord had given him that "America shall be saved!" So, we echoed that loudly with triumphant rejoicing. "And we are here to decree that God is accelerating! And we are here to break up fallow ground. And we are here to go deep in the soil of America, to the curses of racism, the shedding of innocent blood, the slavery issue, the Native American broken covenants, and all the sin, and all the immorality, and all the legislating God out of America's life, but we are here to rise up and say we are going to stand in the gap and say what He says and time is about to catch up to His decree. ... The old is gone away, the new is here to stay! Your glory now will reign! The curse is broken, the curse is broken, the curse is broken! Shout it! Religion can't control! The curse is broken! The curse is broken! ... God is hovering over this nation to begin a Third Great Awakening! And it's going to begin over here in these Carolinas! And the East coast of America is going to burn with holy fire! And the fires of awakening, the fires of revival are coming to this land! You are going to burn in the high schools, the junior high schools, the college campuses, the streets of America, and the churches of America. And we say holy fire! Abundance of rain! Strong wind from heaven is coming to this nation!"

I cannot tell you fully how deeply moved I was to be in this electrifying gathering. We were indeed the Lord's ekklesia, His legislative assembly. The decrees that were released were historic. Scripturally we cannot move forward past our last disobedience without repentance. 2 Chronicles 7:14 (NIV): If my people, who are called by my name, will humble themselves and pray and seek my face and turn from their wicked ways, then I will hear from heaven, and I will forgive their sin and will heal their land. Zechariah 1: 3b (NIV): 'Return to me,' declares the Lord Almighty, 'and I will return to you,' says the Lord Almighty. 1 John 1:9 (NIV): If we confess our sins, he is faithful and just and will forgive us our sins and purify us from all unrighteousness.

We were left with a charge that "New Wells, New Altars, New Fire, New Oil, New Beauty" would need to be opened up and poured out. I thought about what would that take, and what would that look like?

Stretching Your Tent Curtains Wide—Harriet Tubman *in Hilton Head?*

I want to end this chapter with the vision that I had in December 2012 at the official beginning of Releasing Heaven Ministries, as it is very relevant to where we are right now as we prepare for this awakening. As I had mentioned, I had traveled to Hilton Head (Beaufort County, South Carolina) with one of our intercessors for a week to rest up before our full launch by spending some really reflective time with the Lord. Now, I had been to Hilton Head several times before, so it really caught me by surprise that when Beverly and I spontaneously started praying one evening, **I began to see a vision of Harriet Tubman actively**

doing things in what was definitely the same place but in a different time period.

I told Beverly what I was seeing, and I asked her to pause for a moment while I grabbed my iPad to find out whether Harriet Tubman had ever been in Hilton Head. It just seemed to be too far South in what at the time surely was "enemy" territory. And to my surprise, I found an article on the United States Army's official website about how Harriet served in the area in a military capacity. She had been called on to gather and train the slaves recently freed by the Union army when they commandeered some of the islands. In one military raid, her team's actions led not only to a military victory but also to the freeing of 700 slaves. The Lord impressed upon me that He was setting in motion a spiritual underground network, one which would stir and awaken those who were almost unknowingly bound, and that this network would impact both the Carolinas and other cities up and down the East Coast.

Another visit to Beaufort County

To sow more prayer into the vision the Lord showed me about the Spiritual Underground Railroad, all who were available from our ministry traveled to Beaufort County in 2016. On the Sunday of our weekend there, we ventured into Savannah, Georgia on a mission to visit the Haitian Soldier Memorial. Brother Venol, who works at the Haitian National Museum in Port-au-Prince, told our team during our mission trip to Haiti in 2015 that the Haitians had loved freedom so much that they actually helped five other nations, including ours, fight for their freedom. We wanted to honor our spiritual family in Haiti by visiting the memorial and offering up prayers of thanksgiving. I found through research that the memorial was in Savannah, Georgia, less than an hour drive from Beaufort. While we were looking on the map at the Savannah Visitor Center to figure out the walking directions to the memorial, our teammate Becky ran over to let us know that we could also make it to the next tour of The First African Baptist Church, which was the oldest African American Church in North America and an Underground Railroad station.

That church was first organized in 1773, but it would be four years later (December 1777) when the church was officially constituted as a body of organized believers. It was amazing to see what an enslaved people were able to build. Some of the original pews still exist and are in the balcony. "On the outside of the pews are markings written in the African dialect known as Cursive Hebrew," our tour guide told us. She further pointed out how the red door of the church along with the Nine Patch Quilt design in the ceiling of the church indicated that this was a safe house for slaves. The Nine Patch Quilts also served during that time as a map and guide informing people where to go next and what to look out for during their travel.

We then went down to the lower level where the finished subfloor was the actual "station" on the Underground Railroad. Our tour guide pointed out how the African prayer symbol outlined by a pattern of holes in the floor actually served as air holes for the slaves hiding below. She mentioned that no records were kept, so it is unknown how many slaves passed through the church. She emphasized how organized and tight the communication was in those days by letting us know that no one has yet found the actual tunnel entrance. Our young hostess further remarked that the story of the Underground Railroad is not just a Black History story, but it is instead a story that the whole church of Jesus Christ should be proud of. It stands as a testimony of true unity for those simply called by His name, who together—whether black or white—served as "lights" in a time of great darkness, each one putting their own lives and the lives of their families at risk to help another. Yes LORD, do it again!

New Fire

In the past few months, I have been thinking about Harriet Tubman and pondering about the vision of the Spiritual Underground Railroad. I was seeking the Lord about whether we were accomplishing what He intended, or was there something more. Even two team members who live in different states started spontaneously sharing about how they had been thinking about the Underground Railroad. Then I felt inspired to share my Harriet Tubman vision with a new friend who told me that there were a few documentaries available on several online video channels. And, indeed, I found one by Vision Video, a Christian Distributor, entitled "Harriet Tubman — They Called Her Moses." The documentary was narrated by Alfrelynn Roberts and featured interviews with leading scholars, Dr. Eric Lewis Williams of the Smithsonian Institute and Carl Westmoreland of the National Underground Railroad Freedom Center. I marveled at the accomplishments of this great woman known to many as Sister Moses.

I also found documents from a National Park Service's Harriet Tubman Special Resource Study that included a quote by Thomas Garrett, an abolitionist and Underground Railroad Station Master in Wilmington, Delaware. The quote originated from a letter included in Sarah Bradford's biography, Scenes in the Life of Harriet Tubman. Thomas Garrett wrote, regarding Harriet Tubman, that he "never met with any person, of any color, who had more confidence in the voice of God, as spoken direct to her soul... and her faith in a Supreme Power truly was great." (The entire letter is online on the website of the Harriet Tubman Historical Society.) There were also testimonies throughout the Vision Video documentary about Harriet's extraordinary faith.

From her life I saw the progression of how the Lord stretched out the curtains of her vision and influence, which is reminiscent of one of my life Scriptures—Isaiah 54: 1-7 (NIV): "Sing, barren woman, you who never bore a child; burst into song, shout for joy, you who were never in labor; because more are the children of the desolate woman than of her who has a husband," says the LORD. "Enlarge the place of your tent, stretch your tent curtains wide, do not hold back; lengthen your cords, strengthen your stakes. For you will spread out to the right and to the left; your descendants will dispossess nations and settle in their desolate cities. Do not be afraid; you will not be put to shame. Do not fear disgrace; you will not be humiliated. You will forget the shame of your youth and remember no more the reproach of your widowhood. For your Maker is your husband—the LORD Almighty is his name—the Holy One of Israel is your Redeemer; he is called the God of all the earth. The LORD will call you back as if you were a wife deserted and distressed in spirit—a wife who married young, only to be rejected," says your God. "For a brief moment I abandoned you, but with deep compassion I will bring you back."

Harriet first achieved her freedom, but her love for her family and her confidence in her God stretched her to readily start the journey back to rescue them. Without knowing ahead of time how to accomplish the task, the Lord supernaturally guided her back on approximately 13 rescue trips, bringing out 60 to 80 enslaved friends and family members. One of the other things she relied on was the Underground Railroad that was already in place, with both white and black station conductors who sacrificially risked their lives and the lives of their families to do justice. She extended her tent curtains more as she also made provision for her freed family to either make it to Canada or start a new life in the North. She also opened her home to anyone in need, and she cared for the aged. Essentially, she built a community. She also stretched her tent curtains even further as she got involved with the other abolition leaders and regional organizations such as American Anti-Slavery Society and the Philadelphia Vigilance Committee. She became the popular topic in publications by William Garrison and Frederick Douglass. She even supported other causes, such as Women's Rights. And when the door completely closed to making any more freedom runs, she answered a call from the Governor of Massachusetts to help the military. From family, to friends, to strangers, to community, to regional, to national, the Lord progressively used her and the skills she had honed along the way.

The Path to Hilton Head

It is interesting that when we traveled to Virginia Beach this past January 2019 to add worship to the prayers we had already added to Rev. Robert Hunt's prayers of dedication for this nation, we also visited the Hampton Roads Naval Museum. There I learned that the Union Navy had launched campaigns that ended up freeing the slaves in Beaufort County. I marveled that out of the very area that the first slave ships arrived to this land, the Lord released the ships of their rescue. The Lord is A Redeemer!

I also remembered a sermon called Divine Providence delivered by a Presbyterian Pastor named Rev. Isaac Shannon that I came across several years back. It was delivered in New Jersey at the 76th anniversary of the Declaration of Independence, July 4, 1852:

"We deem it appropriate to this day—the Seventy-sixth Anniversary of American Independence—to acknowledge the gracious dealings of God with this nation. We regard our past history as an index to our future destiny. What God has already wrought in this land is the pledge of still greater things to come. He has planted and prospered this nation for important purposes, and those purposes may be learned, in part, from our past history and present condition. It becomes us then not only to acknowledge His providential care in general, but to study the peculiar dispensations of His providence, with a view to determine our present duty, and our future destiny among the nations of the earth. God evidently designed to produce a new type of national character, more vigorous and intellectual than any which preceded us. Men born in three quarters of the world met and struggled upon the American soil. Representatives of ten different European nations, aided by enslaved sons of Africa, contended with the wild men of the forest for possession and for mastery. Long and bravely did the Indian defend his hunting-grounds and the graves of his ancestors. But whatever be his future destiny, he has left an indelible impression upon American history and American character. His history is mingled with ours— written in letters of fire and blood, which attest his courage and his patriotism. The African, too, has made an abiding impression upon our institutions, our system of legislation, and our national character. Present providences indicate that God will overrule both the wrongs of the Indian and the bonds of the African, for the highest good, both temporal and spiritual, of those respective races; and that this nation shall yet prove a blessing to those whom she has oppressed."

Looking back, it seemed that God already had a plan to begin to answer that prayer with the Emancipation Proclamation, the social and civil rights movements over the past 100 years, and again, our meeting of His ekklesia in Columbia, South Carolina. We have made proclamations, but as history shows us, it takes a warring to fully enter into all that God has in store for us. We have an enemy with whom we wrestle that is not flesh and blood, and he hates all that God stands for.

Looking ahead

While looking back and ahead, I believe my prophetic encounter with Harriet Tubman happened because her life and walk carries lessons for us all. Those lessons began with her family and her relationship with her God, lessons similar to those I gleaned from Nehemiah. The lessons then shifted to concerns of the community and then to broader national issues—war and women's rights. And she forged a path for us though she did not have the best of life circumstances: she was a woman, enslaved, disabled, and rejected by her first husband. She lived most of her life in poverty, yet she stands as a national hero, a monument to faith, hope, love and the goodness of our God.

I believe the Lord is touching these same themes as He awakens His people to what He is doing in the earth right now. He is freeing us from captivity to religious spirits and false doctrine; He is equipping us to use the gifts He has given us to address the needs of the people around us. He is enlisting us in His army for broader purposes beyond our immediate sphere—helping those we may not directly know, those who would not know us to repay us—giving freely because it concerns Him and His kingdom.

CHAPTER 18

A Crown of Glory—For the Display of His Splendor!

A Testimony from Haiti Mission Trip

I HAVE AN APOSTOLIC LEADER-FRIEND WHO TAKES the time to dream with God when He gives her a new territory. She asks, "What would this location look like if God designed it?" Amongst other things, the Lord told her in 2010 to go see about Haiti after their devastating earthquake. So, she did. I was blessed to travel with her there, and I have seen the miraculous transformation that she dreamt of—clinics, orphanages, schools, and businesses. Yet, her victories do not mean there has not been trouble.

I traveled there with her and her high school students, along with another glorious sister in the Lord named Angel (real person) in 2013. My friend asked me to come and train an evangelist, whom they supported, in how to pray for her nation. We were three days into the trip before we even traveled to this evangelist's location, and then 30 minutes away from leaving her location before they were able to find her. In that encounter I watched the Lord touch her heart with understanding about His love for her and for Haiti.

She then told me the story of how the Lord saved her on the day of the earthquake. Angel and I had a young translator with us and we listened intently to them both, as by this point she was very expressive and overflowing with contagious joy. She told us how on the day of the earthquake she was home when she heard a voice tell her to leave her house. She obeyed that voice and went to the local store for a few items. As she was leaving the store, the earthquake hit and she watched as her house collapsed under the shaking. She knew she would have been killed along with the thousand others that perished that day. At the time we met her, it had been nearly four years since the earthquake, and she was still homeless. Life had been hard, but when she found that someone agreed with how she really felt about the Lord— that no matter what, God is a good Papa—she rejoiced. So, I turned on our mp3 player and small sound box, and with great joy and expressive worship, we exalted Him and declared that Jesus was Lord over Haiti and invited Him in. And to all of our amazement, the Presence of the Lord walked into the room on our highway of praise. You could tangibly feel Him as He moved into the room step by step. Our young translator gasped as he, too, felt the Son of Man walk in; then the Lord's goodness tangibly filled the atmosphere. Our evangelist invited us to come back and bring our team to worship with her and her community. So, we did; we sent a team to do an outdoor crusade in 2015 and another church joined us.

Since then, there have been more natural disasters and even riots, yet there is continued increase. In 2016, we sent a team to Leogane, the epicenter of the earthquake, to pray with another apostolic leader, also a woman by the way. And I told her that what I saw were festivals in the streets where dance was taken back as worship for the Lord. Her ministry has since done that. And there have been more riots. But God has not changed his mind about Haiti; He told me that she is the jewel of the Caribbean in His eyes.

When we dream with God, we have to dream big. We also have to know that victory and triumph do not mean the absence of trouble. He told us to be of good cheer when we face trials and tribulations because He has overcome the world. If He has overcome, then we have overcome. No sorrow, no sighing, no sickness, no disease happens when He fully returns. And though we long for that day, only those who believe Him will enter into that reality. So, we still have work to do to demonstrate who He is.

Letting life flow to and through our crown

He has given us all seeds of destiny. And for those of us who already believe in Him, He has grafted us into His covenant so we can be like Him—a seed produces after its own kind (Genesis 1:11). And scientifically, when a seedling is grafted into a root, it takes on the characteristics of the root. And we have now also seen some of our lineage that is already in the tree trunk through the still living testimonies of those who have gone before us—the synergy of the ages—their story is our story. But, to help us really blossom and have that "crown of garland, that crown of beauty" with "leaves for the healing of the nations" and with "fruit" that will nourish and sustain others, we need to embrace Holy Spirit. Jesus said it was better for us that He go away, because He would send Holy Spirit (John 16:7). He told us that Holy Spirit would teach us, lead us, guide us, and empower us (John 14:26, 16:13; Luke 24:49).

Holy Spirit also gives great gifts for us to use, and we receive different variations of these gifts, as I simply believe that requires us to stay in community with one another (1 Corinthians 12:4-6). The gifts of the Spirit include wisdom, faith, healings, miracles and prophecy. Romans 8 tells us that we cannot even lead Godly lives without Holy Spirit. I remember how freeing it was for me when I came into that understanding. "It is the Spirit who gives life; the flesh is no help at all. The words that I have spoken to you are spirit and life." (John 6:63, ESV). Without a daily, every-moment type of, walk with the Spirit who gives life, we rub each other, and certainly the world, the wrong way. The love, joy, peace, kindness, forbearance, gentleness, faithfulness, goodness, and self-control that people long to see is fruit of the Spirit (Galatians 5:22-23).

One of the main gifts of Holy Spirit is prophecy. Scripture tells us that all should desire to prophesy (1 Corinthians 14:1, 39). The Word of God truly is alive, active and full of power (Hebrews 4:12 paraphrased), but something explosive happens when the Word is touched by the Spirit of prophecy. Prophecy helps us to tap into the revelation that our God, Creator of the universe, is still unfolding. Our God, our Heavenly Father, longs to show us so many things. Scripture tells us that His thoughts and ways are so much higher than ours, so much beyond our comprehension, our imagination (Isaiah 55:8-9), yet He beckons to us to call upon Him so He can show us great and mighty things (Jeremiah 33:3).

Isaiah 40:25-26 (ESV), To whom then will you compare me, that I should be like him? says the Holy One. Lift up your eyes on high and see: who created these? He who brings out their host by number, calling them all by name; by the greatness of his might and because he is strong in power, not one is missing.

Psalm 8:1-4 (ESV), O Lord, our Lord, how majestic is your name in all the earth! You have set your glory above the heavens. Out of the mouth of babies and infants, you have established strength because of your foes, to still the enemy and the avenger. When I look at your heavens, the work of your fingers, the moon and the stars, which you have set in place, what is man that you are mindful of him, and the son of man that you care for him?

Again, we have to seek that revelation out. The Lord spoke to the multitudes in parables; but when the disciples gathered to ask what the parables meant, He spoke to them plainly. Disciples draw near. "You shall seek me and find me when you seek for me with your whole heart" (Jeremiah 29:13 NIV). Note these additional

Scriptures: "The secret things belong to the LORD our God, but the things revealed belong to us and to our sons forever, that we may observe all the words of this law" (Deuteronomy 29:29, NIV); "it is the glory of God to conceal a matter; to search out a matter is the glory of kings" (Proverbs 25:2, NIV).

So prophecy is the way the Lord shows us portions of what is on His mind, what is in and on His heart, who He is, what He has planned for us—be it through fresh revelation from a Scripture, a dream, a vision, a riddle, a song, an impression, an internal voice, a message through an angel or another person, nature, a knowing, or an audible voice. His heart is to walk this journey together with us and to then spend all of eternity with us—wow!

Another way we get to know what is on His mind and heart is to co-labor with Him. Jesus died on the cross not only to bring us into reconciliation with our Heavenly Father, but also to bring back dominion over the earth—to Him and all of those in Him. Thus, we get to redeem the earth with Him. He left us with two commissions: to go and preach to the lost—to tell them the good news, to heal them, deliver them and teach them to be disciples; and then we are also to make disciples of all nations. We get to go on search and rescue missions to invite our "family" to His banqueting table, and we also get to dream with Him; we get to transform a territory into the way He would have designed it.

So, my scroll ends with an open vision that depicts where I believe overall the Body of Christ is at in this new era that we have crossed into. We are coming into stretching our tent curtains out wide just as Harriet Tubman did when she was called upon both to build a community and to build a nation. The nations are God's idea. Within them are the different fragrances and bouquets that make His garden spectacularly beautiful both now and for all eternity.

The Trumpets Are Sounding! Ride the Wind!

I had an open vision during a Worship and Prayer Gathering on the first Friday of January 2018. In that gathering were leaders of various social justice ministries. I was asked to help direct intercession for breakthroughs for those issues. Initially our worship was reaching high but not piercing into the heavenlies. So, I released a sound. Shortly after that, I sensed a shift in the atmosphere over our city. And to my surprise, I watched in the spirit realm as an angel clothed in white with a blue sash appeared about a half a block away and began to blow a silver trumpet upward (Num. 10:1-10). I waited before sharing that, as I wasn't really sure whether prophetic visions were embraced there and I wanted to see how the vision would unfold.

As the evening progressed, I then saw a company of 8-10 angels dressed in white with blue sashes but with gold trumpets gathered above our city's major crossroads, blowing down into the streets. I could hear the voice of the prophet that often stands near that intersection shouting out, "Jesus saves!" And then liquid gold began to run down the hill upon which our business district and government center sit. In those moments, the worship transitioned to singing about the blood of Jesus, seemingly on cue from an unseen conductor orchestrating. I saw that blood roll out up the hill over top of the gold on the sound waves of the worship. I was then quickened to prophetically sing "Ride the Wind, He loves us."

After the vision started, I had a sense that the group of leaders there were actually meeting in a tent from Revolutionary War times and that we were military strategists (generals and other senior leaders) conferring on how to take the city. When I started hearing "Ride the Wind", I thought about Captain James Jack whose statue was just a few blocks away. Captain Jack was the rider who took the Mecklenburg Declaration of Independence "on the wind" to Philadelphia to present it to the delegates there at the time of the birthing of our nation.

I later remembered that Chuck Pierce and Dutch Sheets called their stop in Charlotte during their 23-City Tour back in September 2017—Unlocking the Winds of Glory in The Carolinas. As I mentioned in the previous chapter, during that gathering, Chuck Pierce released The Wind – a new prophetic mantle – filled with Holy Spirit and led by Holy Spirit. This is the wind that came in Ezekiel 37 from the four corners of north, south, east, and west until it became a vortex, a tornadic wind of heaven, the wind that began to breathe upon dry bones and cause them to come together and be filled with life, such that they became an exceedingly great army. Then Dutch released The Voice of the Lord —His Voice to create, to birth, to resurrect, to bring direction, and to judge His enemies.

Dutch later also hosted a Turnaround Conference in Washington, DC on February 22nd, 2018 (Isaiah 22:22) to usher in this new era of Awakening, which many had been prophesying. There were even many prophecies about how the homegoing of "General" Billy Graham (which had happened the day before that conference) would be a signpost; Billy Graham would leave behind a double portion of his mantle for MANY to carry a portion. And then in March, on the morning of Billy Graham's funeral, as our team headed north to the birthplace of two of our founding fathers, George Washington (General of the American Revolution and our first President) and George Mason (father of the Bill of Rights), there was a wind that came through the Carolinas that shook the entire Northeast.

After several promptings by Holy Spirit to get an understanding of what the blue sashes were about, I did a Google search and found an excerpt from Tim Sheets' book, <u>Angel Armies: Releasing the Warriors of Heaven</u>. That excerpt indeed contained a revelation of angels with blue-colored sashes. I realized I had a copy of that book so I quickly scrambled to find it. I had paused reading the book before I reached that chapter. Apostle Tim noted that blue (the color of a sapphire) represents God's heavenly throne as well as Holy Spirit.

There also are several Scriptures that are significant for this vision:

Numbers 10:1-4 (NIV): "The Lord said to Moses: 'Make two trumpets of hammered silver, and use them for calling the community together and for having the camps set out. When both are sounded, the whole community is to assemble before you at the entrance to the tent of meeting. If only one is sounded, the leaders—the heads of the clans of Israel—are to assemble before you.'" There is a remnant, a leadership, which is first being awakened. The Lord gave Chuck Pierce the term "triumphant reserve."

Revelation 1:9-13 (NIV): I, John, your brother and companion in the suffering and kingdom and patient endurance that are ours in Jesus, was on the island of Patmos because of the word of God and the testimony of Jesus. On the Lord's Day I was in the Spirit, and I heard behind me a loud voice like a trumpet, which said: "Write on a scroll what you see and send it to the seven churches: to Ephesus, Smyrna, Pergamum, Thyatira, Sardis, Philadelphia and Laodicea." I turned around to see the voice that was speaking to me. And when I turned, I saw seven golden lampstands, and among the lampstands was someone like a son of man, dressed in a robe reaching down to his feet and with a golden sash around his chest.

The lampstands here are the leaders of the churches. The voice like a trumpet is the Voice of the Lord, the golden sash and robe represent authority. And as seen in Isaiah 22:22, the Lord's authority is Sovereign. Isaiah 22:20-22 (NIV): "In that day I will summon my servant, Eliakim son of Hilkiah. I will clothe him with your robe and fasten your sash around him and hand your authority over to him. He will be a father to those who live in Jerusalem and to the people of Judah. I will place on his shoulder the key to the house of David; what he opens no one can shut, and what he shuts no one can open."

Eliakim, the son of Hilkiah, was governor of the palace (financial minister) for Hezekiah. His name means whom God will raise up, or resurrected one. In Revelation 3:7-13, we see Jesus describing Himself in His letter to the church of Philadelphia, using these words about being the one who holds the key of David that opens, and what he opens, no one can shut, and what he shuts no one can open. Jesus is the One with the final authority, which is now communicated through Holy Spirit. And it was significant for me that the Blood of Jesus was over the gold in my vision. (1 Peter 1:18-19, NIV).

This vision denotes the Lord's wake-up call. The trumpets are sounding! He is speaking, and angelic help under the authority of Holy Spirit has been activated. It denotes that the Lord is laying claim to all that rules our atmosphere, be it business, government, the church, or any social justice cause. But He wants to confer with us—there is a tent of meeting, of discussing and formulating strategies. The Vision indicates that Worship and Prayer are catalysts for seeing and hearing this help from God. Of note, the dreams, visions and prophecy depicted in Joel 2, Acts 2, and 1 Corinthians 14 are a part of city-wide transformation. As we "ride the wind", we need to remember that, as believers, we belong to another kingdom (John 18:36)—we are supernatural—we are a kingdom of priests and kings (1 Peter 2:9); when led by Holy Spirit, we function as sons of God (Romans 8:14). And we have a dual mandate, to preach the gospel to all people (Mark 16:15), and to disciple nations (Matthew 28:19), to reform society by administering provision and good government, opening doors that no man can shut and shutting doors that no man can open.

Demonstrations

In addition to our normal Strategic Prayer Outings and Ephesians4Movement (E4M) Equipping Services, we purposed to specifically and directly respond to the angelic visitation over our city. We formulated two major outreach clusters: first, Kids Praise in the Park and Relationship Building Activities, and second, Releasing Joy in Our City— Outdoor Worship & Prayer Watch in an Uptown park venue.

What's in your house?

Kids Praise in the Park and Relationship Building Activities

Two immediate things that we heavily looked at in planning a response to the angelic vision were: first, recognizing that the Lord had already transitioned us for our E4M Services to the First Ward of Uptown Charlotte; and second, what did we already have in our house? For anything family oriented, we always looked to two of our Senior Leaders, Kevin and Rosemerry. They were already primed and trained for awakening and revival in the Lord's core kingdom building block— families.

We held several internal strategic planning sessions and then forged ahead with demonstration activities for children in our community which we called "Kids Praise in the Park." We also planned other relationship building activities to help families create and strengthen their support networks, namely a biblically-based equipping session, a roundtable info session at Imaginon (Children's Library), and a Worship and Prayer Watch focused on the family.

Releasing JOY: The Power of Ministry Alignment & Bridging the Generations

Our second outreach cluster centered on welcoming Holy Spirit afresh into our region by purposely engaging other ministries for combined strength, and by targeting the Millennials who now lived in the many condos and apartments that had sprung up in Uptown Charlotte. We endeavored to be a voice to the generations to demonstrate the church responding to social justice causes and to demonstrate church leadership positioning itself to build solid relationships across the generations.

Again, looking to what we "already had in our house", our format was one of a Worship and Prayer Watch. The Lord provided us with a generous donation to rent one of Charlotte's main outdoor venues. We planned, prayed, extended invitations, and prepared the ground. As a part of our invitation to other groups, we asked that they devise a way to follow-up with folks, and then have some activity or event already planned (within the next month or so following this outreach) that they could invite folks to. For Releasing Heaven Ministries, we planned two follow-on Watches in November and December that everyone could attend.

In our planning efforts, we also heeded the prophetic word from Chuck Pierce about lying low and being circumspect during the June-October timeframe. So we did not advertise the outreach beyond our personal associations and the ministries the Lord had highlighted. For preparation, our Ephesians4Movement (E4M) Equipping Services for July, August and September focused on providing: training in Prophesying; a knowledge base about Mindsets and Worldviews of the generations; and sharing testimonials about Revival and Awakening.

Finally, we also held a Strategic Prayer Outing at Reed Gold Mine, the site of the nation's first gold rush, as the angelic vision I had shown gold being liquefied and running downhill from our center square. Uptown Charlotte is literally on a hill, and there are gold veins that run underneath the city's streets.

Prayer Targets for City and Region that were covered by the various organizations included, a Welcome to our Heavenly Father, Jesus and Holy Spirit; praying for City and Regional Leaders; Awakening and Revival; Families; The Generations; Our Identity in Christ—Sonship; the Marketplace; Creativity: Arts; End Homelessness; End Human-Trafficking; the Carolinas being One by God's original design (North and South Together!); the Nations— those who had come into our area as well as missions outward: Prayer being a centerpiece of every home; and then for Salvation.

Ride the Wind!

We watched the Lord use these activities and events (and our prayers even spanning back 20 or more years) to inspire the participating groups and the general public to look beyond themselves and their normal routine to the care of the community-at-large. We watched as more collaboration, more creative solutions, and even more prayer efforts began to spring up everywhere. There is even a national effort underway to promote city-wide transformation. Personally, our connections with several churches and various non-profit organizations addressing issues such as human trafficking and homelessness deepened. And we are thrilled that the Lord has stretched wide our curtains to see the generations aligned and women arise. We even launched a new marketplace prayer watch, and we also continue to prayer-walk colleges and universities throughout the Carolinas.

Finally, new harvest fields beyond our region have also sprung up. In addition to our global mission to the Kurdistan region, we have built relationships with ministries functioning in Kenya, Greece and other Caribbean islands. We are currently in the throes of planning our participation in outreaches and gatherings in Maryland, Pennsylvania and Delaware. And our team has been delighted to see other ministries press into this new apostolic-prophetic era. One group that particularly touched my heart was a group of young African American missionaries serving in Youth With A Mission (YWAM) stepping into an Isaiah 19 call to Egypt, Assyria and Israel – wow!

Isaiah 58:6-12 (NIV): Is not this the kind of fasting I have chosen: to loose the chains of injustice and untie the cords of the yoke, to set the oppressed free and break every yoke? Is it not to share your food with the hungry and to provide the poor wanderer with shelter— when you see the naked, to clothe them, and not to turn away from your own flesh and blood? Then your light will break forth like the dawn, and your healing will quickly appear; then your righteousness will go before you, and the glory of the Lord will be your rear guard. Then you will call, and the Lord will answer; you will cry for help, and he will say: Here am I. If you do away with the yoke of oppression, with the pointing finger and malicious talk, and if you spend yourselves in behalf of the hungry and satisfy the needs of the oppressed, then your light will rise in the darkness, and your night will become like the noonday. The Lord will guide you always; he will satisfy your needs in a sun-scorched land and will strengthen your frame. You will be like a well-watered garden, like a spring whose waters never fail. Your people will rebuild the ancient ruins and will raise up the age-old foundations; you will be called Repairer of Broken Walls, Restorer of Streets with Dwellings.

Isaiah 61:1-4 (NIV): The Spirit of the Sovereign LORD is on me, because the LORD has anointed me to proclaim good news to the poor. He has sent me to bind up the brokenhearted, to proclaim freedom for the captives and release from darkness for the prisoners, to proclaim the year of the LORD's favor and the day of vengeance of our God, to comfort all who mourn, and provide for those who grieve in Zion— to bestow on them a crown of beauty instead of ashes, the oil of joy instead of mourning, and a garment of praise instead of a spirit of despair. **They will be called oaks of righteousness, a planting of the LORD for the display of his splendor. They will rebuild the ancient ruins and restore the places long devastated; they will renew the ruined cities that have been devastated for generations.**

PART FIVE:

Conclusion — The Trumpets are Sounding!

THE LORD HAS PROMISED ME THAT HE IS ANSWERING my prayer. My heart-felt cry, belted out at age 29 on the sidewalk of a park in West Philadelphia, was to see His transforming power in full operation. Now is His Pre-appointed Time! The angels are in motion and the trumpets are sounding! I challenge you that if you have not already done so, that you would answer the Lord's clarion call to awaken. It is a simple "Yes, Lord! I will ride with You."

Below are some signposts and quick reminders on what to continue to watch for as you enter into this Greatest Great Awakening, the Greatest Holy Spirit Outpouring that the people of God have ever seen.

Keep your eyes on God's first nation Israel; we have been grafted into His covenant. After nearly 2000 years, Israel has been back in her land for at least 70 years and, since 1967, has Jerusalem as her capital. The fullness of the Gentiles is approaching. Keep an eye on ministries, such as Glory of Zion International, which have the Ephesians 2 "One New Man" mandate as a part of their vision. These ministries typically are very in tune with the heart and eternal plan of God. Similarly, keep an eye on ministries that are pursuing the Isaiah 19 prophecy: remember God's Genesis 17 promise to Abraham. Consider sowing a portion of your finances into a ministry that is functioning in Israel. And pray for Israel, bless her; pray for the peace of Jerusalem.

Be mindful of how the Lord governs His kingdom. He has all authority and He has directed us to be baptized in fire by Holy Spirit to be empowered to serve Him (Luke 24:49). And He has called some men and women to share in his leadership anointing—some apostles, some prophets, some teachers, some evangelists and some pastors to equip believers for the work of ministry (Ephesians 4:11-16). Align yourself with an apostle who is within your "tribal giftings" as Holy Spirit leads. Remember the Tabernacle in the Wilderness—the Lord had Israel encamp around the tabernacle in their own tribe and then in a company with at least two other tribes. Their giftings achieved a strategic blending that benefited the whole nation. And align with others across the Body of Christ to form a community of support. This alignment does not have to be formal; simply pray for one another and be aware of one another's vision, mission and activities to provide support as Holy Spirit leads. One of the important things to be watchful for is rivalry. I have been so thrilled to see several senior leaders in the Body of Christ on the same platform together. They have recognized that there are times when convergence is needed.

1 Corinthians 3:4-6 (NIV): For when one says, "I follow Paul," and another, "I follow Apollos," are you not mere human

beings? What, after all, is Apollos? And what is Paul? Only servants, through whom you came to believe—as the Lord has assigned to each his task. I planted the seed, Apollos watered it, but God has been making it grow. To the contrary, we are called to esteem one another with higher honor.

Lastly, occupy! The Parable of the Gold Coins or Minas or Talents in Luke 19:11-27, and another in Mark 13:32-37, which is about the Master who went away to a far country and left his servants in charge, both speak to me about planting your seeds of destiny, using your gifts and authority, being watchful in prayer, and being a good steward. I would also add here the need to continually remember history—the synergy of the ages; to expect angelic help; to have faith in the promise and character of God: He has made covenant with you.

Even dry bones can revive. Even those who have been in bondage: you are being called up. Those who have been in the wilderness, those hidden ones, the triumphant reserve: you are being called up. And to those for whom this is your 11th hour: come, come into the harvest fields.

Now is the Pre-appointed Time—the Trumpets are Sounding! Like Abraham, Moses, Joseph, Esther, Jesus, the Waldensians, the Moravians, Rev. Robert Hunt, the pastors of the congregations who helped establish the colonies, Harriet Tubman, Papa Seymour, Rev. Dr. Martin Luther King, Jr., Archbishop Benson Idahosa, John Gimenez, Derek Prince, Billy Graham, the apostles and prophets of today and the believers of Jesus throughout the ages, follow the passion of your heart. Plant your seeds of destiny in the Lord's covenant root. Allow Him by His Spirit to nurture you for the display of His splendor to become an Oak of Righteousness for your family, your city and your nation: "Rebuild the ruined cities and repair the devastations of many generations." Holy Spirit and the Angel armies are once again positioned, and the Lord is with you in the tent of meeting! Stay rooted, stay aligned, stay awake, and build His kingdom: Ride the Wind!

Spirit of Mecklenburg— Statue of Captain James Jack. His ride in 1775 with the decrees for freedom to the newly forming seat of government helped kindle the embers of revolution!

END NOTES

Chapter One

Concussion, written and directed by Peter Landesman (2015; Culver City, CA: Columbia Pictures, 2016) DVD.

Jonathan Zimmerman, "Philadelphia Riots, 50 Years Later." *Pittsburg Post-Gazette*: PG Publishing Co., Inc. 24 August 2014. Web. 25 March 2019. https://www.post-gazette.com/opinion/Op-Ed/2014/08/24/Philadelphia-riots-a-half-century-later/stories/201408240053

Chapter Nine

The Covenant: the Story of My People. Original Musical by Elizabeth and Robert Muren, Presented by International Christian Embassy Jerusalem, Charlotte, NC, 26 April 2007. Performance.

"Jewish Biographies: Nobel Prize Laureates (1901-2018)," Jewish Virtual Library. Web. 25 March 2019.

David Brooks, "The Tel Aviv Cluster." *The New York Times*: The New York Times Company. 11 January 2010. Web. 25 March 2019.

Chapter Ten

MorningStar TV (Joyner, Rick). (2013, December 6). *#FreedomOfReligion.* [Video File] Retrieved from: https://www.

morningstartv.com/prophetic-perspective-current-events/freedom-religion

Chapter Twelve

Anne Gimenez, "Washington for Jesus." https://www.afj2012.org/index.php/army-of-intercessors/123-washington-for-jesus

The Forerunner. "Washington for Jesus 1988." http://www.forerunner.com/forerunner/X0619_Washington_for_Jesus.html

Chapter Fourteen

Vinson Synan. "The Lasting Legacies of the Azusa Street Revival." *The Enrichment Journal*: The General Council of the Assemblies of God, 2019. http://enrichmentjournal.ag.org/200602/200602_142_legacies.cfm

Etgar Lefkovits. "Nehemiah's wall uncovered." *The Jerusalem Post*: Palestine Post Ltd. 28 November 2007. Web.

Adam Pivec, "Nehemiah's wall discovered." *Biola Magazine*: Biola University. Spring 2008. Web.

Gail Wallace, "The Queen & The Cupbearer Connections between Esther & Nehemiah." The Junia Project. 12 May 2015. Web. https://juniaproject.com/queen-cupbearer-connections-esther-nehemiah/

Chapter Sixteen

"Crusade City Spotlight: Charlotte, NC," Billy Graham Library Blog. 23 May 2012. Web. https://billygrahamlibrary.org/crusade-city-spotlight-charlotte-nc/

Session #5 (2/24/2018 @ 9 AM), Turnaround Conference, Dutch Sheets Ministries. Washington DC, USA. 2/22-24/2018. Livestream.

Chapter Seventeen

Also see reports on Releasing Heaven Ministries Blog: www.releasingheaven.org

Herbert Spaugh, Episcopus Fratrum, "A Short Introduction to the History, Customs and Practices of the Moravian Church," Hope Moravian Church, Winston Salem, NC. Web. http://www.hopemoraviannc.org/MoravianChurch.htm

"James McGready, Presbyterian Minister, 1763-1817," Historical Foundation of the Cumberland Presbyterian Church and the Cumberland Presbyterian Church in America. Web. http://www.cumberland.org/hfcpc/McGready.htm

Ruth Quinn, "Harriet Tubman: Nurse, Spy, Scout," United States Army. 27 May 2014. Web. https://www.army.mil/article/126731/harriet_tubman_nurse_spy_scout

Harriet Tubman: They Called Her Moses, directed by Robert Fernandez (2018; Worcester, PA: Vision Video 2018) DVD. https://www.visionvideo.com/dvd/501822D/harriet-tubman-they-called-her-moses

"Harriet Tubman Special Resource Study: Environmental Assessment," National Park Service, United States Department of Interior, November 2008. https://parkplanning.nps.gov/projectHome.cfm?projectID=11008

Rev. Isaac N. Shannon, "Divine Providence in American History and Politics: A Discourse delivered in the Second Presbyterian Church, New Brunswick, New Jersey, July 4, 1852," Ackerman, A. (Publisher). Available via HathiTrust Digital Library (Public Domain) https://hdl.handle.net/2027/loc.ark:/13960/t07w6tc6z

RESOURCE LIST

A Time to Triumph by Chuck D. Pierce

A Time to Advance by Chuck D. Pierce with Robert and Linda Heidler

The Messianic Church Arising! by Dr. Robert D. Heidler

The Apostolic Church Arising by Chuck D. Pierce and Robert Heidler

The Future War of the Church by Chuck D. Pierce and Rebecca Wagner Sytsema

God's Unfolding Battle Plan by Chuck D. Pierce

The Spiritual Warfare Handbook by Chuck D. Pierce with Rebecca Wagner Sytsema

The Apostolic Woman! by Linda Heidler with Chuck D. Pierce

The Queen's Domain: Advancing God's Kingdom in the 40/70 Window by C. Peter Wagner

An Appeal to Heaven by Dutch Sheets

Giants Will Fall by Dutch Sheets

Releasing the Prophetic Destiny of a Nation by Dutch Sheets and Chuck D. Pierce

The Power of Praise and Worship by Terry Law with Jim Gilbert

True Stories of the Miracles of Azusa Street and Beyond: Re-live One of The Greatest Outpourings in History that is Breaking Loose Once Again by Michelle P. Griffith and Tommy Welchel

Azusa Street: They Told Me Their Stories by J. Edward Morris and Cindy McCowan, narrated by Tom Welchel

Angel Armies: Releasing the Warriors of Heaven by Tim Sheets

ABOUT RELEASING HEAVEN MINISTRIES TEAM

Just as the Moravians of old set The Lord's Watch, and the Charlotte militia forged the Hornet's Nest for the sake of freedom, Lord we declare that we, your ragtag militia, this small company of your Triumphant Reserve, will defeat our enemies through strategic prayer and worship, disrupting their communication and permanently binding their influence and advancement; and we O Lord receive the strength of Your Hand and the help of Your warring angels who fight on our behalf as we advance Your Kingdom and enter into the Promises you have ordained for us!

Email us at e4m@releasingheaven.org for a free Watch Guide to transform your city!

Follow us on Facebook and Instagram

Visit our website and blog at www.releasingheaven.org

ABOUT THE AUTHOR - YVONNE DENISE

Yvonne is a Native Philadelphian, but is a Sent-one to the Carolinas. She has been active in ministry for nearly 40 years, serving both in the marketplace and in the local church. She is a watchman intercessor who walks in the anointing of a seer prophet. In the past, she has served in youth ministry, led ministry and prophetic prayer teams, helped lead a bible college, taught on revival and the Abrahamic covenant, and has been on several mission assignments. In addition to having a certificate from a bible college, she holds a Bachelor of Science in Economics degree in Entrepreneurial Management and Political Science from The Wharton School, University of Pennsylvania and a Master of Arts degree in Organizational Communication from Queens University of Charlotte.

Yvonne is the Founding Apostle of Releasing Heaven Ministries (RHM). She is aligned as a House of Zion and Ministry of Zion under Glory of Zion International (GZI). She is also aligned with Global Spheres Inc. (GSI) as an apostolic network member. She is recognized by GSI as an Apostle-Prophet. Her heart passions are to labor to see every home become a house of prayer, to be a bridge connecting the generations, and to be a catalyst for women arising to their God-ordained calling. She regularly shares her God Stories on social media under "This Is That: Makin' It Plain," and she regularly writes blog posts for Releasing Heaven Ministries (RHM) at www.releasingheaven.org.

Her itinerary can be found at www.ephesians4movement. org, or you can write her at e4m@releasingheaven.org.